How to
Invest *in*
Rental
Properties
Without Mortgaging Your Soul

Mabel Armstrong

Stone Pine Press

Published by
Stone Pine Press
PO Box 585
Marcola OR 97454

This publication is designed to provide information to the reader on the subject covered. It contains the opinions and ideas of the author. It is published with the understanding that the publisher and author are not rendering legal, accounting, investment, or other professional service. If professional advice is required, the services of a certified professional should be sought.

Where Stone Pine Press was aware of a designated trademark claim, that designation appears in initial capital letters.

Edited by Vickie Nelson
Design and production by Niki Harris
Cover Design by Opus 1 Design

Publisher's Cataloging-in-Publication Data

Armstrong, Mabel
How to invest in rental properties without mortgaging your soul/Mabel Armstrong.

Includes index.
Bibliographic references

ISBN: 0-9728929-0-7   HD1382.5 J348
Library of Congress Control Number: 2003095643   332.63'24-dc21

06 05 04 03 5 4 3 2 1

Attention professional organizations, corporations, universities and colleges:
Quantity discounts are available on bulk purchases of this book for educational or gift purposes, or as premiums. Special book excerpts can also be created to fit specific needs. For information, please contact Stone Pine Press, P.O. Box 585, Marcola OR 97454.

Contents

Part Five: How to Be a Landowner

Preface

The Eight Reasons I Own Rental Properties

1. I want tangible investments. I want something I can look at, touch, show off to friends and family. Unlike other tangible investments such as gold or silver, I want an investment I can enhance by my own actions.

2. I want an investment I can understand. If I pay attention to local rents and sales prices, I can figure out what I should pay for property and what I should charge for rent. I can talk to mortgage lenders and find out what they charge for loan costs and interest in my area. The stock market feels like smoke and mirrors to me. After following the performance of big-name market analysts in the bust of 2000 and 2001, I'm not convinced any amount of study would have helped me understand the market.

3. I'm a controller. I want investments I can control. When I buy rentals I control the condition of the properties as well as tenant selection, rents, and most of the financial aspects.

4. I want to contribute to my community. I believe everyone deserves a safe, secure, attractive, comfortable place to live. It gives me great pride to offer tenants the cleanest, safest units I can. My small portfolio of socially responsible mutual funds may contribute to the causes I care about, but I won't see that reflected in my own community. My rentals reflect my values to my community.

5. I want to make a living, not a killing. I can keep my rents below market so more people have access to my units. I like the challenge of figuring out how to support myself comfortably and still supply affordable housing to my community.

6. I love the creative aspects of remodeling and fixing up. From the challenge of trying to squeeze a workable bathroom into minimum space to working out color schemes and landscaping, my involvement with my rentals satisfies my need for creative outlets.

7. I enjoy the environmental aspects of saving existing buildings and turning them into assets to the community. I like preserving the history and look of older neighborhoods. I enjoy the challenge of recycling building materials, both from my own projects and others.

8. I like the money. Every month thirty people write checks to me. What's not to love?

Introduction

A few years ago, I was so poor that I decided which bills to pay every month by throwing them all up in the air and paying only those that landed on the coffee table. I thought this process gave all my creditors an equal shot at my meager bank balance. It was not a happy time in my life.

Now, when the first of the month rolls around, I smile as I think about all the people who are writing checks to me. I made one decision that turned my financial life around: I decided to take active control of my finances. My first goal was to begin to provide for my retirement.

It took me a while to settle on rental property as the best investment for me, and I had much to learn along the way. I learned that I have no aptitude for property management, actually tenant management. I fired my first two property managers. I learned to hire my own termite and dry rot inspectors. The list goes on.

My education in rental owning has been enormously profitable. I was able to retire early, my rentals now produce half my income, and my real estate portfolio is worth about $2 million. The biggest surprise for me was to learn that I love owning and working with rental property. Now I want to share my enthusiasm with you and convince you that rental housing is a terrific investment.

From my first duplex, purchased in 1986, I progressed to owning 34 individual rental units distributed in buildings as diverse as a 100-year-old farm house and a new 12-unit complex. In the process I've invested less than $50,000. That sounds like a lot of money, but it was invested over a ten-year period, and my tax savings on my teaching salary covered most of it.

How do you make this happen for you? How do you get 34

people to send you a big check every month—well, actually send your property manager a big check every month—and the IRS to reduce your income tax by 30 percent or so?

When you own rental property, both of these unlikely scenarios happen. People happily pay your mortgage payments, and the IRS reduces your income taxes by a considerable amount. On top of all that, the value of your investment increases monthly. You have the pride of owning properties, and you get the opportunity to contribute to your community in many ways.

What This Book Is   This book is the result of my desire to share what I've learned, in the hope that you, too, will come to experience financial independence. It is a hands-on manual for day-to-day use in your first real estate adventure. In Part One I'll try to dispel some of the horror stories you may have heard about rentals, and show you why owning rental property is your best investment bet.

In Part Two you will learn how to set your investment goals, develop plans, and find professional advice. You will also learn how to find rentals that fit your plans.

Part Three will help you calculate the amount of cash you'll need and give you some ideas about where to look for that cash.

Part Four will help you figure out how to get more cash out of your rentals, first without selling. Then, if you decide to sell, I offer ideas about why, when, and how to sell to your best advantage.

Part Five offers some tips and strategies to help make your ownership of rental property successful, satisfying, and reflective of your values. Chapter 15 speaks directly to women in hopes of reducing the disproportionate number of women represented in the elderly poor.

Buying rental properties, managing them, and reselling involves stacks of paperwork. You will be more confident in your first few transactions if you have had a chance to look over the paperwork before your lender or escrow agent hands it to you. To give you a chance to preview the standard documents involved in real estate transaction, I have included Internet site addresses where you can find sample documents at the end of the appropriate chapters.

Other forms, particularly those you should begin working on before you're ready to buy a rental, such as a financial statement, I've included in the appendix. These sample forms are representative of those you will come across as you begin your investment career and do not include much of the "small print" found on standard forms. They will, however, alert you to the kind and amount of information you will need to supply.

I hope this book will become your own personal guide to prosperity, a gift from me to you.

What This Book Is Not   This is not a get-rich-quick scheme. Investing in rental properties requires patience, thought, and a fair amount of your time in the beginning. Successful investing in real estate requires ongoing commitment to learning about investing, studying your local markets, and minding your investments.

It is not a formula book. Formulas work best for the people who write books about real estate investing by formulas. This book is about investing in small rentals, the process I know a bit about. Even with small rentals, every market is different, and every property within a market is different. No formula fits all circumstances.

This is not a textbook on the theories of real estate investing. I don't know much about those theories, and I'm not sure I believe the little I do know. Investment theories are developed by economists, and I subscribe to the theory that "If all the economists in the world were laid out end to end, they wouldn't reach a conclusion."

How to Use This Book   To get the most out of this book, you should treat it like a cookbook. As with a new recipe, read it all the way through rapidly. Then go back and start over. The second time through have a pencil, notebook, and calculator at hand. Work through the examples until they make sense. Fill out the forms and self-tests. Make notes in the margins and use high-lighters to call out information you may want to refer to later.

Take your time Reflect on the information in the book and the information you generate with the exercises. Try using the examples with the real estate advertisements in your Sunday paper. Give yourself time to consider how the ideas apply to you. Read and ponder a bit every day. You'll be glad you did. In short, make this a working book for your rental investments.

Go online Look at the web sites listed at the end of the chapters. On the Internet you can:

- Use net worth forms and find out how much you really can invest.
- Get a professional assessment of the real estate market in your community.
- Find out how much the average rental sold for last month.
- Look at sample loan applications and learn what information a lender will want.

Finally, this book does have numbers in it. However, the arithmetic never goes beyond fifth-grade level addition, subtraction, multiplication, and division. At all times you should be able to follow the examples easily and compare the conclusions with your own market and your financial goals. If you can figure out your car's gas mileage, you can do real estate math.

I think the way to get from trying to figure out which bills to pay every month to depositing rent checks from others, is to invest in small rental properties. I hope to show you how to start small, grow at your own pace, and finish with your golden years really golden. You are on your way to a new view of the world of finance, a view that I hope will benefit both you and your community. It will be an exciting journey. *Bon voyage.*

Mabel Armstrong
October 1, 2003

Part One

Why Own Rentals?

Chapter 1

Face *Your* *Investment* Fears

Confront the Myths About Real Estate Investing

You must do the thing you think you cannot do.
ELEANOR ROOSEVELT

What thoughts pop into your head when you think about owning rental properties? Do you shudder over 3 a.m. telephone calls about overflowing toilets? Do you think about friends and co-workers who bought high, sold low, and lost a "bundle"? These stories are part of what I call the Myths of Real Estate

These myths weren't created deliberately by people who want to keep you out of the market. More likely they arose, in part, from the invisibility of real estate transactions. People don't invest in real estate online, or follow their investment value in the daily newspaper. The process is hidden from the average person, and that makes it mysterious.

People who have had bad experiences because they made easily avoidable mistakes also contribute to the myths. And the perception that owning real estate means owning the Sears Tower convinces many that real estate is not the investment for them.

Eight Myths About Real Estate Dispelled

The eight major myths of real estate investing are these:

1. You need lots of cash to invest.
2. You have to be super smart, or have an MBA, to invest in real estate.
3. Banks only loan money to people who have lots of money already.
4. You will have to spend huge amounts of time managing rentals.
5. The process is so complex and confusing the average person can't understand it.
6. The insiders, big boys, and high rollers get all the good deals.
7. Landlords are bad people who abuse their tenants, the community, and the environment.
8. You need to be a real risk taker to invest in real estate.

Let's look at these myths one at a time and see if there is any truth in them. Some myths, you'll see, are based on a rational fear of losing money or time. Others come from a fear of the unknown. As you read through this book, you'll find chapters that tell you what to expect from buying and renting property. As the unknown becomes known, your fears will begin to disappear.

Other sections will help you learn techniques that will maximize your gain and avoid mistakes that could cost you time and money. For now, here are my thoughts about these myths.

Myth 1: You Need Lots of Cash If you are in the market for the Sears Tower, you will need a hefty down payment. If you are starting out by buying a duplex, however, I will show you that lack of cash should not keep you out of the market. First, I'll show you how you can buy a rental for far less cash than you might have believed. Secondly, I'll teach you how to calculate the exact amount of cash you will need for a purchase. Finally, I'll suggest some strategies for finding the cash you need.

Myth 2: You Have to Be Super Smart or Have an MBA to Invest in Real Estate My real estate teacher liked to remind us that every piece of property is owned by someone. Some of those ones are, of course, big corporations with armies of accountants on staff. But most rental owners are average people like you and me.

Look around you. Do you think the guy who owns the duplex down the street is any smarter than you are? Probably not. If he could learn to do it, you can learn to do it, and this is just the book to help you. That brings us to college degrees.

You don't need a degree in anything in order to successfully own and manage rentals. You do need to learn all you can about all aspects of buying, renting, and managing property.

Real estate, as taught in most business schools, is very theoretical. MBAs may know all about international finance, but most of them don't know a thing about your local real estate market. The MBA will have to do the same homework you do.

You actually have an advantage, because you know you need to learn about the process, while the new business graduate may think he or she knows it all. Formal education, particularly in business, often gives people a false sense of security. The purpose of this book is to help you figure out what you need to know, help you learn the basics, and point out ways to continue learning.

Myth 3: Bankers Won't Lend Money to People Who Need It There is a grain of truth to this myth. Bankers and mortgage lenders want to insure that they will get the money they lend back with interest. They tend to make new borrowers jump through hoops to guarantee they have the resources to continue paying off a loan, even if the rental market goes down, or the borrower faces some other financial problem. The solution is to work on your financial documents so that you appear to be a person who will repay a loan according to the lender's needs.

Unfortunately, obnoxious loan officers do exist, those who forget that their employer won't make money if they refuse to loan it.

When my friend Debra wanted to buy a house, she encountered just such a person. The loan officer she talked to looked at her earnings and meager savings and announced, "Forget it. You'll never be able to buy a house." Debra was so traumatized that she left the bank in tears and never again considered buying her own house.

I believe a good financial advisor could have helped Debra figure out how to get a house. She may have needed to spend a couple of years of tight budgeting and careful searching for the right loan program and the right house. But there is no reason she could not have found a house and a loan that fit her circumstances. Unfortunately, Debra was so crushed she won't even talk about her dream of owning her own home.

These days most lenders use some sort of rating process and lend money only to those who achieve a particular score. Depending on the lender, the requirements may seem pretty obscure and the process interminable. You can speed up the process by establishing a relationship with a lender before you need the money. Be sure to discuss the lender's requirements and put some time into satisfying them. Chapter 5 suggests ways to develop this relationship, and Chapter 8 will help you get your documents in order so your loan request will be hard to turn down.

Myth 4: You Will Have to Spend Huge Amounts of Time Managing Rentals Many of us would like simply to give some money to a financial advisor and say, "Take this and make it multiply and don't bother me with the details." We certainly don't want to spend our scarce time managing our investments. And it's true that some rental owners do spend enormous amounts of time attending to the details. Others choose, as I have, to hire a professional management organization to do that for them. The choice is yours.

I'll talk more about the pros and cons of professional management in Chapter 5. For now, let me say that for seven percent of gross rent my managers screen and interview all tenants, collect rents and deposits, inspect units before tenants move in and after they move out, pay all bills including mortgage payments, handle all maintenance including the 3 a.m. leaking toilets, and even take me out to lunch every couple of months. There is no way I could do all that for what I pay them if I wanted to do anything else with my time. The best part is that the management expense, like all others, is tax deductible.

Myth 5: The Process Is Too Complex for the Average Person to Understand Real estate transactions are complex, and from the outside the process may even look like magic. However, as science fiction writer Arthur C. Clarke once remarked, "Any reasonably advanced technology will look a lot like magic to the uninitiated."

We're all uninitiated in many areas. I can't begin to imagine how you program a computer to launch a space shuttle, and I'm not sure I could learn to do it. I have no doubt, however, that you can learn how to buy a rental and make it pay off.

One reason investing in real estate looks like magic is that much of the process of buying and selling property is hidden. Once you find a piece of property and write an offer, the Realtor shuttles between you and the seller interpreting each of your responses to the other. Your loan documents disappear into a black hole in the lender's office. The appraiser sends the appraisal report to the lender, not to you. The loan officer disappears with your application and spends six weeks "processing" it. No wonder it feels like magic. All these people are doing things about your financial future behind closed doors and out of your sight.

Some of this is deliberate. My favorite escrow officer tells about the deal that went sour during closing when the buyer commented that the first thing she intended to do was get rid of that "awful carpet." The seller was so furious at the insult to her taste that she tore up the documents and refused to sell the property.

People can get emotional when they are buying or selling personal residences. The professionals try to keep amateur buyers and sellers from messing up deals. So they keep them away from each other and often close them out of the negotiations.

You, however, are working on becoming a professional. If you make it clear to Realtors, bankers, and others that you want to learn, you can expect better treatment. If you ask good questions and let these professionals know that you consider them to be part of your team, you should get a very different response. If you continue to feel shut out of negotiations or decisions, find a different professional.

Throughout this book, I'll suggest ways to make sure you are part of the process. After several deals, you should be directing most of the transactions.

Myth 6: The Insiders and Big Spenders Get All the Good Deals

Unless you really are after the Sears Tower, you will find that you have an advantage over the high rollers. First, there is less competition for the kind of properties you want. The guy making an offer on the Sears Tower is not interested in the duplex you want.

Secondly, you know your market in a way he never will—which makes you the insider. Take the example of the big developer who looked at my market back in 1992. Rents were up, vacancies were down to about two percent. Wow! What a great place to make lots of money. So, the big developer put up a 100-unit apartment. Unfortunately, he thought he could rent his one-bedroom units for $750.

Had he researched the market, he would have realized that $750 was luxury-apartment rent in this town at that time. And his location was one that appealed almost exclusively to college students who can't, or won't, pay $750. His big fat development was 50-percent vacant for a year, at which time it went into receivership.

If you've studied your market and know what rents for how much, you won't make this kind of mistake, and you'll have a big advantage over out-of-town developers.

Insiders are another matter. You just have to learn to live with them, and hopefully, outsmart them. The insiders are usually employees of real estate firms, the folks who hear about good properties first. Of course, they want to snap up the good deals. In Chapter 5 you'll learn how put together a team that will help you get the inside information.

Joining a rental-owner organization is one way to get some of that information. After all, the folks who own the rentals are the ones who will sell them. The information about who is selling often makes the rounds of other owners long before a Realtor hears about it.

Myth 7: Landlords Are Villains Who Abuse Their Tenants, Their Communities, and the Environment Nearly everyone has experienced the Landlady from Hell. But we've also experienced rude waiters and surly clerks. Part of taking control of our lives is deciding not to let those people define who we are and how we behave. The existence of nasty people certainly doesn't mean you must become one of them. Here is your chance to show the world there is a better way.

Both the Preface and Chapter 3 speak to my view of the ethical way to own and manage rental properties. Not only do I think you can model socially and environmentally responsible ways to own and manage property, I think you should do just that.

I don't think profit is a dirty word. You must make a profit if you are to stay in business. Throughout the book I'll describe ways to increase the gain from your rentals. At the same time, I'll talk about ways to increase the contribution your rentals can make to your community.

Myth 8: You Have To Be a Risk Taker to Invest in Real Estate The level of risk in a real estate investment depends on the decisions you make at the time you invest. As with other investments, choosing the path of least risk is also choosing the path of least return.

The only way I've found to deal with risk is to look at all sides of the question, then decide which possibility I find most risky. Although I listed the myth that you must be a risk taker to invest in real estate last, I think the fear of losing money is the primary reason more people don't invest in rental properties. Let's look at this fear in more detail with an example.

Four Real Estate Investment Strategies

Sarah, Jessica, and Caitlin, all teachers, each inherited $100,000 in 1997. Because they define risk differently, they chose different investment strategies. Sarah was a prudent investor who did careful research and put her money in a well-regarded mutual fund. She settled on a well-diversified portfolio, just as cautious analysts advise. Because she didn't need cash at the time, Sarah reinvested her dividends. By the end of 1999, Sarah's investment had gained 16 percent in value.

Jessica wanted a more tangible investment. She decided to buy a rental, but was uneasy about borrowing money to make the investment. She bought a $100,000 duplex, paid cash for it, and now owns it free and clear. She rents the units for $500 a month. After subtracting expenses, Jessica realizes $9,000 a year cash flow, or net income, from her investment.

Caitlin bought four similar $100,000 duplexes. She paid 25 percent down and borrowed $75,000, for 20 years, at eight percent interest on each one. Caitlin rents her duplexes for $500, just as Jessica does, and experiences the same operating expenses. Caitlin's four duplexes produce $48,000 a year in rent. But because she makes mortgage payments, she banks just $7,045 a year from rents.

Caitlin and Jessica also enjoy the tax benefits of owning real estate. They each deduct depreciation on their rentals and Caitlin gets to deduct the interest on her mortgage payments—$6,750 per duplex for a total of $27,000. Added to the depreciation on her four duplexes, about $14,000, Caitlin deducts about $41,000 from her rental and teaching income. The tax saving added to her cash flow gives Caitlin $21,000, beyond her salary, every year.

Until the middle of 2000, things looked good for all three sisters.

■ *Four Investment Strategies*

Investment	Leverage (loan size)	Benefits	Risks	Comments
1. Buy one house for cash	No loan; no mortgage payment	Highest cash flow; lowest risk	Slower equity growth; highest case requirement	Good option for older people
2. Borrow to buy house or duplex	Up to 20% down; modest leverage	More rapid equity growth	Modest risk; higher down payment; breakeven or small positive cash flow	
3. Buy duplex, 4-plex, or larger complex	90% to 100% loan (aggressive investment)	Lowest cash for entry	Requires private mortgage insurance	Possible negative cash flow
4. Buy fixer house or duplex	This option depends on the circumstances. It can produce the highest return, but requires special skills and temperament.			Best for younger people

Then came the bad times. By June 2001, the value of Sarah's stock portfolio had dropped three percent. The tragic events of September 11, 2001 drove the market down even further. By the end of 2002, the value of Sarah's mutual fund had dropped a total of 18 percent.

A table comparing the returns Jessica and Caitlin get from their investments is in the Appendix. The table shows that both Jessica and Caitlin realized nice returns from their investments at a time most of their friends were playing the stock market. Jessica's total yearly return was 15 percent and Caitlin's about 35 percent. Caitlin's loans reduced her immediate cash flow, but increased her total return and paid off at tax time.

Jessica and Caitlin also experienced the downturn that started in 1999. Because they live in an area where high tech drove the economy for the previous decade, unemployment rose, and they both experienced vacancies. For Jessica, one empty unit is a 50-percent vacancy. However, she does not make mortgage payments, so she can reduce her rents to attract and retain tenants. She can compete strongly with owners who have large debt service, or mortgage payments.

Caitlin would be in serious trouble if she had not put 25 percent down on her purchases. Her debt service is only $600 per month per duplex. She can lower her rents to $400 per month, make the mortgage payments, and still have some cash left over for maintenance. Actually, given the large tax breaks her investments provide, she could probably drop her rents even further and weather the rough times just fine. If her duplex rented for $500 a couple of years ago, advertising it for $375 now would have people flocking to her door. She would have less to put in her pocket every year, but she would survive. And her tenants would continue to pay the mortgage.

Anyone Can Buy Rentals, Should You?

How much risk are you comfortable with? Risk is like beauty—it's in the eye of the beholder, and we all have our own idea of the kinds of financial actions that make us uncomfortable. Financial advisors like to say, "Don't exceed your comfort level." Do you know how much risk you are comfortable with?

When I was starting out, I didn't know my comfort level. My real estate instructor gave me the best handle on it. He said, "If you wake up in the middle of the night in a cold sweat thinking, 'What have I done?' you haven't exceeded your comfort level. Every prudent person has moments of dread when making decisions about large amounts of money. However, if you wake up five or six times a night, you have exceeded your comfort level."

Risk and profit are opposite sides of the investment coin. Jessica's investment choice was less risky than Caitlin's, but it also limited her income. Caitlin could have made another choice that would have increased her income, but it would have also increased her risk. She could have made much smaller down payments and bought more units. If she had been able to buy duplexes for only 10 percent down, she could have bought twice as many, and had twice as much income—$90,000 per year.

However, smaller down payments mean larger loans, and larger loans mean larger payments. A loan of $90,000, for 20 years, at nine percent, has a payment of $810 per month. Rents of $1,000 per month and expenses of $250 would leave Caitlin with only about $750 each month to make the $810 mortgage payment. If the economy turns sluggish, she will find it hard to raise rents in order pay the bills, and she wouldn't be able to afford to lower rents to attract and keep tenants. Even if the economy is steady, she will have months where she will have to dip into her teaching income to support her investment.

Each investment decision is based on choices like those made by the three women. The risk in the choices, however, can be weighed as we saw the three sisters weighing them. If you are a risk-avoider, you might buy a rental outright and not borrow money. Or, you might use a very large down payment and borrow just a small amount. Or you might find a couple of friends to join you in the venture and spread out the risk.

If you are on the far end of the risk spectrum—a real adrenaline junkie—you might put as little down as possible and take out loans as large as the lender will make. Even Caitlin didn't go that far. By the standards of real high flyers, she was a wimp. The way you define risk is completely personal. No one can do it for you. You'll get a chance to assess your own risk tolerance in Chapter 4.

Few of us are good at predicting the future. The crash of the dot.coms and bio-technology stocks certainly proves that, and real estate markets are only slightly more predictable than stock markets. However, while people don't need to buy your Enron stock, they always need a place to live. You may not be able to sell your duplex for what you want when you want, but the rent keeps on coming. That makes owning rentals less risky than many other investments.

The big advantage in real estate is that the investor—you—has lots of control. You decide what to buy and how much to spend. You could buy a single-family home for all cash with no loan. Or you could borrow a couple of million dollars for an up-scale, high-rise apartment building. Or you could do something in between.

You control your investment plan. You can, as my brother and sister-in-law did, buy a small house to rent and stop there. They had some cash and wanted a rental for investment. They bought a very modest house in Seattle for about $89,000. I was shocked at the price, since at that time that amount of money would have bought two houses where I live. Then they sank $25,000 into it fixing it up.

Clearly, they knew the market better than I did. They rented it the first day they advertised, and have kept it full from day one. When they refinanced last year—seven years later—the house was appraised at $289,000.

At present my brother and sister-in-law don't plan to buy any more rentals. The sales market is still overheated, but rents are dropping rapidly, not the market in which to buy rentals. For them, the buy-and-hold strategy is just what they want right now. But they could change their minds at any time. They have lots of equity and could use it to increase their real estate portfolio. Even as the real estate sales market drops, they have a tangible investment that provides cash flow, equity increase, and tax shelter.

Finally, like most other things in life, you need to enjoy real estate in order to make it pay off. You probably have the personal attributes necessary, or you wouldn't have read this far. If you find you have no inclination toward real estate, don't waste your time with it. Find something that really motivates you. You can't make money if you're not enjoying life.

Summary

✔ You can buy rental property with modest amounts of cash.

✔ You don't need advanced degrees or a Mensa-IQ to be a successful rental owner.

✔ You can learn to make lenders say yes to your loan request.

✔ You can decide how much time you want to spend managing your rentals.

✔ You can build relationships that will help you get inside information on good buys.

✔ You have an opportunity, as a rental owner, to contribute to your community.

✔ You can adapt your investment strategy to match your risk tolerance.

■ *On the Internet*

Find out what Uncle Sam can do to help you buy a rental at **www.hud.gov**

Chapter 2

Rental Properties: Your Biggest Bang

Buy land, they ain't makin' any more of it.
WILL ROGERS

Most of us want more money. Whether it's to send the kids to college, travel to exotic places, or buy that new boat, most of us want more money than we can squeeze out of our paychecks alone. We intend to budget for future needs with savings accounts, CDs, or mutual funds, but somehow, between paying our bills and buying groceries, our good intentions remain just that. Many of us worry that we will never realize our dream of a comfortable retirement.

Take a moment to imagine what your life will look like when you are 65. Close your eyes and picture yourself reading the paper as you sip from a hot mug. Are you sipping gourmet tea or coffee? Or are you drinking coffee bought on sale at the warehouse grocery? Can you afford a sweet roll to go with it? Are you planning a trip while you enjoy your coffee? Or, is the only trip you can afford a walk in the park? Now, consider what the life you want will cost when you are 65 years old. Will your investments provide that life for you?

What Your Investments Should Do for You

Your investments will be the vehicle that carries you toward your goals. Good investments give you the best chance of arriving at your personal and financial goals. Most of us want to find investments we can get into with fairly small amounts of cash, have limited risks involved, and pay off reasonably well. If we add the requirements that we are able to study and learn about the market and that we as investors have some control over our investment, the number of good investments is limited. I believe that small rental properties meet all the requirements for a quality investment. My own experience is an example of the way rental properties can pay off for you too.

Little Cash Required for Entry A little more than fifteen years ago, I was a single parent, working as a teacher. I had recovered from the debts left from my divorce, but I still spent most of my paycheck every month, and I had made no financial plans for retirement. Following the advice of a financial planner who said I should diversify, I invested in some stocks, oil, a real estate limited partnership, and gold. The only person who made money on my investments was the man who sold them to me. By 1986 the value of these sure things was less than half of what I had put into them. At the time I put my hard-earned money into those losing ventures, another financial advisor told me, "Women should never own rental properties. They just don't have the skills to manage rentals." Fortunately, these experiences made me so mad I signed up for a real estate investment class at the local community college. There I heard what I needed to hear: Yes, it's doable. Yes, you can do it. Yes, you can do it on a shoestring. Yes, you can figure out before you buy what kind of cash flow you can expect.

I bought my first duplex for about half of what it had originally cost to build. It had been repossessed by the bank and had stood vacant for several months. The property was being vandalized and the bank could see the value decreasing. They wanted to sell, badly.

My closing cost for the duplex, including down payment and loan fees, was less than $4,000, and I paid that with my credit card. A little belt-tightening at home and a quick cosmetic redo of the duplex, and in a couple of months the rents were paying off the mortgage, the maintenance, and the credit card.

This first venture paid off so well that I bought the duplex next door a couple of months later, using the same technique. Within three years I had purchased six duplexes, each time finding *distressed properties*, those in need of improvement. I used my willingness to patch walls, paint, and clean to acquire a property for very little cash. I was on my way to financial independence.

Limited Risk I expect that like most of us your idea of the worst-case investment risk is that you would lose all of your money. When you buy rental properties, the possibility that you will lose all of the money you invest is very small. A rental property is a *tangible asset*; you can touch it. While it is true that real estate sales and rental markets are cyclic, even in a slow market prices seldom drop 40 percent as the Dow did recently, and, unlike bankrupt corporations, your asset continues to exist. You may not be able to sell your duplex immediately, but your renters will still be paying the mortgage and giving you a positive cash flow as well. You will even be able to sell your duplex eventually, while no one will ever again buy your Enron or World Com stock.

The second fear that comes to mind for most people is that you won't make as much money as you could have in a different investment. Perhaps if you had been one of the lucky people who bought tech stocks at the right moment, then sold at the right moment, you would have made loads of money. In general, however, when you balance the advantages of rentals—income from rents, tax shelter, and equity increase, against other investments—I think you, too, will prefer rentals to stock-market roulette.

Much of the risk associated with buying rental properties has to do with the amount of money you borrow. Choosing to borrow a little or a lot depends on you and your goals. Borrowing a lot increases your risk. However, you can position your investments to decrease the risk. Your dedication to learning about the process of rental property purchase and management and to studying your own local real estate market will go a long way toward minimizing your risk.

The profitability of real estate investments depends on your knowledge of the real estate market in a particular location. You have a much better chance of understanding the real estate market in your own community than you have of understanding the intricacies of international monetary exchange, biotechnology, or pork belly futures. Knowledge of your market alleviates a great deal of the risk involved in buying rental properties. When you own well-placed rentals, you can take comfort, as I do, in knowing that even when the sales or the rental market slows, your rentals continue to exist and the rents continue to come in.

The Four Ways Rentals Pay Off

Your investment in rental properties has the potential to pay off in four ways: cash flow, appreciation, equity buildup (debt reduction), and tax shelter.

Cash Flow is money available for you to spend after the costs of the investment are paid. This is income, a little like dividends from stocks. In Chapter 1 we saw that both Jessica and Caitlin had cash flow from their rentals—the money left over after their expenses were deducted from the rental income.

Appreciation is the increase in the market value of your investment. Obviously, this increase depends on your local real estate market, which normally continues to increase. Fortunately you have some control over the market value of your property. If the market places a premium on well-kept, attractive yards and buildings, you can maintain and enhance the condition of your properties, adding substantially to their value.

Equity is the difference between the market value of your property and the debt against it. If you own a property free and clear, your equity equals its market value. If you borrowed money to buy the property, your equity equals the difference between market value and your mortgage balance. As you pay off the debt, using your rental income, your equity increases. Both the market increase and the mortgage decrease add to your equity in your rentals.

The magical part of investing in rental properties is that your renters are actually paying off your debt and increasing your equity. If you maintain attractive rentals with competitive rents, you will find people lining up to help you pay off your loan. Just try to find someone willing to help you pay for stocks you bought on margin.

Tax Shelters are specific categories of deductions that help you lower some of the tax you pay to the IRS. Mortgage interest and depreciation on your property are two tax shelters provided by rentals. In the chapters on buying and selling, I'll illustrate some of the ways you can use tax shelters to increase the return on your investment.

A specific tax-shelter advantage of real estate is depreciation. The IRS allows you to deduct a percentage of the original cost of the property from your gross income each year, on the assumption that buildings have a finite life span and are "wearing out." Real estate provides one of the major tax shelters recognized by the IRS. In Chapter 4 you will see how Jessica and Caitlin used the depreciation deduction to reduce their taxes on their teaching salaries.

Uncle Sam Will Help You Buy Rentals

There is more good news for those who invest in rental properties. If you qualify for an FHA-insured loan and are willing to live in one of your units, you may be able to finance your purchase with as little as three percent down. That is, if you move into one side of the duplex you buy, you could buy a $100,000 rental for as little as $3,000 down plus closing costs. You could live rent free while your renter/neighbor makes the mortgage payments for you. The FHA program extends to four-plex properties, meaning you might be able to find and buy a four-plex for as little as three percent down.

Lending institutions classify properties of fewer than five units as residential—rather than commercial—and make residential loans on them. You can buy four-unit properties using residential loans, those with the lowest down payment and lowest interest rates available.

Leverage: Use Other People's Money

Borrowing money to buy stocks or consumer items can be a recipe for disaster. Using a lender's money to launch your investment career in real estate can, on the other hand, make a lot of sense. The use of borrowed money to increase your purchase power is called *leverage*. A physical lever allows you to multiply mechanical force many times. Financial leverage allows you to multiply your financial

■ *Leverage Gets Your Rental off the Ground*

Cost of Rental = $100,000

$25,000 Cash but No Leverage   **Leverage of $75,000 Loan**

force many times. Let's see how this operates in real estate.

Caitlin used the leverage of other people's money to buy four duplexes rather than just one. She borrowed a total of $300,000. Such a large loan may sound really scary to you, and it *is* a lot of money to owe. But Caitlin expects her investment to pay off.

The table below shows how Caitlin's loan helped her leverage her inheritance into a higher total value than either Sarah's or Jessica's. If each sister had gotten a seven percent return each year, this is how their investments could compare at the end of the first year.

■ *Comparison of Investment Value at End of One Year*

	Sarah Mutual Funds	Jessica 1 Duplex	Caitlin 4 Duplexes
Initial investment	$100,000	$100,000	$100,000
Value at end of one year	107,000	107,000	128,000
Total increase in value	7,000	7,000	28,000

Each duplex increased $7,000 in value. Caitlin has four duplexes, so her increase in value for the $100,000 she invested was $28,000.

If real estate continues to appreciate at seven percent a year in their community, Jessica will have one duplex worth $140,000 at the end of five years. She will have made 40 percent on her investment over that time period, and she will have enjoyed added income in the meantime.

Caitlin has enjoyed all the advantages of a good investment as well: cash flow, a larger tax shelter than Jessica's, and the addition of equity to her net worth as she pays off the loans. She didn't have as much direct cash flow as Jessica. What has increased is her equity. By using her original $100,000 as down payment and borrowing money to buy four duplexes, she has amassed a real estate portfolio worth $561,000, more than half a million dollars. That's leverage!

Return on Investment Many investors like to calculate the return on their investment as a way to track the performance of their rentals. That calculation for our three sisters also shows the advantages offered by buying rental property and borrowing to do so.

■ *One-Year Return on Investment*

	Sarah Mutual Funds	Jessica 1 Duplex	Caitlin per Duplex	4 Duplexes
Cost	$100,000	$100,000	$25,000	$100,000
Cash flow	reinvested	9,000	1,476	5,904
Appreciation	7,000	7,000	7,000	28,000
Tax savings	0	662	662	2,648
Principal reduction	NA	0	4	16
Return on investment	7%	17%	37%	37%

The calculations for the table above are in the Appendix.

You can see from the table that buying rentals paid off better in the first year than mutual funds, even at seven percent return, the stock market's 50-year average. And borrowing to buy rentals paid off even better.

As it turns out, however, much of the return on rentals is not immediately spendable. Which brings us to the next issue.

Getting Cash Out of Rentals

One of the risks investing in real estate does carry is that it's hard to turn rentals into cash rapidly. Real estate is *illiquid*. However, I think this is where investing in real estate gets to be really creative. For example, if at the end of five years Caitlin needs cash, she has numerous options since she has built up a good net worth in that time. She could:

- Sell two duplexes and pay off one of the remaining two entirely, so she would own one free and clear. Then she would have mortgage payments to make on just one. She would then clear $9,000 a year as cash flow plus the $1,350 she gets from the duplex with the mortgage. She would also have realized at least $80,000 cash on the sale of two of her rentals. Of course she would owe taxes on both the rental income and the capital gain from the sale. Still, $80,000 cash ain't bad. She would have made back all of her original investment and more and would still have two duplexes.

- Refinance one, two, or more duplexes and use the tax-free cash for anything she chooses. Refinancing would increase her monthly debt service and increase the balance she owes on the loan. However, she might use the money to purchase another property for cash with the thought that the cash flow from a free and clear property would cover her increased debt service. The money from a refinance is tax free, a big point to remember.

- Sell one, two, or more duplexes and buy a big—12 unit or larger—apartment building. Cash flow increases directly with the number of units per building, and Caitlin could sell one property, buy another, and defer the capital gains tax. This process is discussed in Chapter 11.

Of course, Caitlin should never sell or refinance without talking with her financial and tax advisors first. We'll look at the details of her options later in this book.

Cover Your Assets: Invest Prudently

All investments include some risk. Even a good investment, the vehicle taking you to a comfortable retirement, can be sideswiped by a reckless driver—a new IRS code, perhaps. You can't avoid all risk. You can, however, decide how much risk you can live with comfortably and what you are willing to risk in order to increase your financial payoff.

Let's return to our sisters. Sarah was the most risk-averse. The long-term stock market return of seven percent seemed reasonable to her. Poor Sarah! Even if the market had not taken a nose dive before and after September 11, 2001, she would not have experienced the payoff that Caitlin did. Prudence now requires that Sarah stick with the market until it recovers.

Jessica and Caitlin both bought rentals. Jessica took the almost risk-free path of paying cash for a rental. Her rents give her an extra $1,000 a month, an amount that will increase as rents in her area increase. For real estate investments, Jessica's route was one of low risk, but also, minimal income. Jessica has some of the same options Caitlin has for getting cash out of her investment, but she will never have access to as much cash as Caitlin.

Realtors like to say that investors make their money on real estate "going in." That means that the investor has thought about what risk he or she can live with, has structured the down payment and terms of the deal to provide what is needed, and has a good idea of what to expect from the investment. In rental properties, two negative possibilities always have to be considered: vacancies or low rents, and decreased sales values. Let's look at the way Caitlin factored in those possibilities.

Although Caitlin might have invested more aggressively, buying more or larger properties, she chose to consider both higher vacancies and a sluggish economy. She expected that her salary would offset small losses she might incur for the following few years.

She calculated that at the end of five years she would have enough equity to sell two duplexes and pay off one entirely. Then, even in a recession, she could lower rents and still have her renters paying off the mortgage on the last duplex. Taking more risk than her sisters did doesn't mean that Caitlin wasn't prudent.

When structuring a real estate investment, a prudent investor asks, "How can I do this so I can weather the bad times *when* they come, as they surely will?" Any investor needs to remember that all markets are cyclic. Rents go up, rents level off, rents go down.

When I bought my largest complex, twelve units, the seller was advertising a one-bedroom unit for $510 per month. He calculated his sales price on the assumption that all twelve units would rent for $510, ignoring the fact that he had four vacancies, which should have told him something. It told me that the property was over-priced, but I believed that I could make the purchase pay.

The seller owned the complex free and clear—he was not making mortgage payments—so he was not especially concerned about vacancies. I, however, intended to finance my purchase and did not believe the small one-bedroom units would support rents that high.

To provide for my assumption that I would have to lower rents in order to fill the vacancies, I paid 40 percent down and borrowed just 60 percent of the purchase price. In the end, I had to lower rents to $435 to fill up the vacancies. To be fair to the existing tenants, I lowered the rent for them also, so the gross income I am receiving for the complex is a full $1,000 less every month than the previous owner calculated.

If I had believed the seller's calculations and borrowed 75 percent of the purchase price, I would be having trouble making the payments, even with no vacancies. As it is, the complex nearly always provides a positive cash flow.

Prudent investors consider these facets of a real estate purchase when structuring a deal. Here are some of the items you should think about, each of which will be expanded on in Chapters 8 and 9.

Purchase Price You may be able to negotiate the purchase price and down payment more easily if you buy a two- to four-unit building from a private party. Corporations or partnerships, which often own the larger complexes, have calculated sales prices to the penny, and the sellers are often not interested in negotiating. That doesn't mean you shouldn't try. Always offer a price that makes sense to you and allows some wiggle room.

Never, *never* let a Realtor tell you your offer would insult the seller. The seller can always reject an offer. Most states require that a Realtor present all written offers, and who knows? You might get lucky.

Terms of the Loan—Interest Rate Most lenders have calculated their interest rates very carefully. They know exactly what they want a loan to yield. The only choice you might have will be whether you want to pay down the interest with additional cash called points— the lender will lower the interest rate if you pay them to do it. You often see lender advertisements stating, for example, "Interest 8 percent or 7.5 percent with 1 point." This means that you can borrow at 8 percent, or you can pay the lender an additional 1 point (1 percent of the loan amount) at closing to get a 7.5 percent loan.

Terms of the Loan—Down Payment and Amount of Loan With her $100,000 Caitlin could have bought up to ten duplexes, depending on how much she wanted to borrow. Consider making yourself a simple spreadsheet like the one below so you can compare down payment and mortgage payments and pick the scenario that fits your circumstances.

Terms of the Loan—Maturity Real estate loans are typically made for 15, 20, or 30 years, and mortgage payments vary accordingly. For example, if Caitlin's loan had been for 15 years, at nine percent, her mortgage payment would have been $751. If she had taken a 30-year loan, her mortgage payment would have been $604.

My friend Jim, who just turned 50, bought a four-plex this spring. He decided on a 15-year loan, although the payment will be more than for a 30-year loan. He wants his purchase to be paid off when he is 65 years old, since he expects the rents will be his major source of income at that time.

Here is a table that shows how the mortgage payment changes depending on the amount of the loan and the time of maturity. The purchase price is $100,000 in each case.

■ *Loan Payments for Loan Amounts and Years of Loan*

Loan Payment = Principal and Interest at 9% on a $100,000 Loan

Loan	Down	15 Years	20 Years	25 Years	30 Years
$90,000	$10,000	$913	$796	$755	$724
80,000	20,000	811	720	671	644
75,000	25,000	761	675	629	604
50,000	50,000	507	450	420	402

This table shows that choosing a particular down payment and length of loan allows you to tailor the details of a real estate purchase to meet many different circumstances. For a $100,000 purchase, the monthly mortgage expense could range from $402 to $913, depending on the amount you borrow and the length of the loan.

As a prudent investor, you will know how much you will be able to pay for monthly debt service long before you make an offer. Chapter 4 will help you set your financial goals so that you have the numbers in mind as you begin to look for rentals.

Summary

✔ Your investments should advance your financial and personal goals.

✔ Rental properties can provide you with cash flow, equity buildup, and tax advantages.

✔ Using other people's money (borrowing) increases the return on your investment.

✔ It is possible to be a prudent investor. Doing your homework will let you invest in rentals and still minimize your risk.

■ *On the Internet*

Follow trends at **www.realtytimes.com**

Check out the market in various cities on **www.HomeSeekers.com** and **www.Homeadvisor.com**

Walk through model homes of a big builder at **www.kbhomes.com**

More sophisticated ideas are at Milt Tanzer's site associated with his book, *Real Estate Investments and How to Make Them.* **www.investmentre.com**

The Wall Street Journal real estate site is at **www.RealEstateJournal.com**

Chapter 3

You Can Do Good As You Do Well

Treat the world well. It was not given to you by your parents. It was lent to you by your children.
KENYAN PROVERB

In the first two chapters I talked about the ways owning rentals can pay off financially. In this chapter I want to describe some less tangible rewards. Depending on your vocabulary, you might call these rewards building good karma, giving back to your community, investing responsibly, or maybe accruing spiritual equity.

Many of us hope to leave the world in better condition than we found it. We work hard at raising our kids to be productive adults and we try to strengthen our communities. Few of us, however, would include owning rental properties in our list of ways to build strong communities. Here's why I think landlords have the power to promote healthy communities and a healthy planet.

Your Community

You cannot walk or drive in any city today without encountering the problem of the homeless. What may not be obvious from the text on the cardboard sign carried by some homeless people is that a large percentage of them are actually employed parents. Although the minimum wage has increased dramatically here and there, it is still not enough to live on. Consider the income of the single wage earner. If a woman makes a minimum wage of $6.50 per hour, she earns $260 for a 40-hour week, or $1,040 a month before taxes. If just 20 percent of that wage goes to withholding taxes, she takes home $832 a month.

From what we get we can make a living. What we give, however, makes a life.
ARTHUR ASHE

Federal guidelines suggest that no one should pay more than 40 percent of their wages in housing costs, or just $333 if the monthly income is $832. How many one-bedroom apartments rent for that? Now consider that our minimum-wage earner may be a single parent. If she spends $333 for rent—40 percent of $832—she has $500 left for expenses for the rest of the month. More likely, she will spend the $500 for rent and have $332 left for clothing, transportation, food, utilities, and all the other expenses we all face monthly.

Paying rent is not the only challenge for minimum-wage workers. Even harder is finding housing in the first place. Since most rental tenants must pay first and last month's rent and a deposit, they must come up with about $1,000 just to rent a $400 apartment. A homeless family of three with one wage earner will find it nearly impossible to come up with that much cash.

This is where you, as a socially aware landowner, come in. The first thing you can do is to consider negotiating for the last month's rent and deposit. Could a prospective tenant manage those costs if the money were spread out over three months or four? Could you increase the rent to $425 or $450 per month with the written understanding that the extra goes to pay off the required last month's rent and the deposit?

Once you realize that some rental "rules" actually help contribute to homelessness, you may come up with creative solutions on your own. And, once you realize that a significant number of the homeless are women with children who have fled abusive relationships, you may be really motivated to find some solutions. Here are a few I like:

Reasonable Rent Helps Everyone I just sold a six-plex in a blue-collar part of town, where my one-bedroom apartments rented for $365. Across the parking lot was another almost identical six-plex. The owner of that complex had been advertising one-bedroom units for $425 for more than a year. For 18 months those units stood empty. The owner was so sure those units were "worth" more that he wasn't going to lose money by lowering the price. Let's see what the numbers really say.

In the 18 months the units have been vacant, that owner has lost $7,650, assuming they had rented at his price. Even if he drops his rent now and rents them at a lower price, he will never make up the amount of money he has lost. Further, he has kept affordable units off the market in an area where they are badly needed. At $365 my units stayed full and I increased the pool of potential tenants by keeping the rents reasonable.

Speaking of affordable housing, be sure to get to know the people at the Section 8 office. Section 8 renters are people on public assistance whose rent is subsidized by HUD, the Department of Housing and Urban Development. I see rental ads all the time that state, "No section 8." I think refusing to rent to HUD clients is a mistake.

My experience has been that Section 8 tenants actually have two people, my manager and their case worker, looking over their shoulders. My manager has a good relationship with the local Housing Authority, and I profit from that relationship. I do have to take care of silly items like a cracked switch plate occasionally, but I know that if a tenant damages something, the Housing Authority is right there when I need them, the check gets to me promptly, and I don't have to run down tenants who skip without paying. Finally, I find Housing Authority tenants far less destructive than many college students.

Rules Make the Residence I'm not suggesting you eliminate rules for financially strapped tenants. All tenants need to abide by the same rules, and those rules must be in writing and signed by all parties. One of the things that means is that all unmarried adults living in a unit must complete a rental application and sign the rental agreement.

The rules need to be designed to protect both the landowner and the tenants. At the same time, they should contribute to making tenants feel as if your rental is their home. For example, many people want pets. My favorite rental cartoon shows a man hauling his cat, wearing fins and a snorkel, out of the flush tank. The caption reads, "You can come out now, Fluffy, the manager is gone."

In my experience, tenants take one of two routes when pets are not allowed. They sneak pets in, like the cat in the snorkel. Or, they don't stay long. If I'm trying to provide housing that tenants will consider home, I have to be willing to take pets. "But what about the damage pets do?" you ask.

Pet damage is an issue you need to deal with right up front. My manager has rules that seem to work well. Tenants may have one cat or a small dog. A small dog is one that weighs 20 pounds or less and is more than a year old. Pet-owning tenants pay a pet deposit with their first rental payment.

Actually, I suspect many tenants have two cats, but I think a cat with company may be less inclined to shred the carpet under the bedroom door than one that is bored out of its mind. Like many other terms of the agreement, there is room for negotiation. If a tenant want two cats, the deposit may go up, or she may be asked to sign a longer lease.

Common sense and the need for tenants to feel at home should be the rule. I think a 50-gallon aquarium on the second floor has far more potential for damage than a second cat. But if the tenant who has lived in a unit for five years wants another cat or a new puppy, we'll talk about it. We will be sure to do an inspection—and provide her with the written report—before she gets the puppy. But I would never want to lose a good long-term tenant over a pet.

The Planet

You probably try to do your best to be environmentally responsible in your personal life: you try not to buy over-packaged materials, you limit your use of toxic materials, and you recycle everything you can. When you own more properties than just your home, you have the opportunity to encourage more people to follow your example.

Landscape Decisions By paying attention to environmental issues associated with your landscaping, you may be able to move away from conventional landscaping practices and all the associated problems: toxic runoff, profligate use of water, and noise and air pollution from all those lawn mowers and leaf blowers.

You probably know that pesticide and fertilizer runoff from the nation's lawns constitutes a major source of water pollution. You can reduce or prohibit the use of pesticides and fertilizers on your own properties, or you can remove lawns entirely. If you replace lawns with native plants, you not only reduce the need for fertilizers and pesticides in the yards, you also reduce the need for water. Native plants have evolved in their environment. They get by with rain alone and don't need additional fertilizer. Unlike lawns, which a friend refers to as "landscapes on life support," natives are self-sufficient.

You can landscape so that you work with nature to reduce the effects of development. Fruiting trees and shrubs attract birds and other wildlife. Well-placed trees can help keep a house cool and reduce the cost of summer air conditioning. Shading roofs and walkways can reduce the temperature around a unit as much as 10 to 20 degrees in the summer. Not only will the air conditioning cost go down, tenants will be happier.

Resource Conservation   Even if your tenants pay for their own water, installing low-flow shower heads is a good idea. High-pressure shower heads often result in water splashing off the showerer and onto the floor, which can cause dry rot. Changing washing machines to front-loading units can save as much as 30 percent of the water used. If the temperature setting on water heaters is lowered to 140 degrees, you may notice immediate savings.

All light fixtures in common areas should have fluorescent bulbs. You may be able to talk your tenants into using fluorescent bulbs also. Your local utility may be willing to underwrite the cost of changing bulbs in individual units to fluorescent. Call to find out.

Provide recycling options for your tenants. Most people really do want to recycle. If you make it easy for them to sort trash and recycle, they will do it. Again, your utility or garbage service may have some ideas. In my area, the garbage service provides the labeled containers and weekly pickup free of charge.

Maintenance   Your own repair and maintenance efforts can have a dramatic impact on the environment. Non-toxic alternatives to oil-based paints are becoming more available. Sources for less toxic paints and recycled construction materials can be found in the yellow pages and on the web.

Perhaps the biggest impact you can have is to do each maintenance job as if you intended it to last. By using long-wearing materials, which may cost more at the outset, you will limit the need to do a repair over and so reduce the amount of waste and the amount of resources used. Doing repair jobs the right way, and for the long haul the first time, ultimately saves money. Many landowners can't see beyond the next month's statements. But, averaged out over a year or two, careful, professional repairs pay off.

Giving Back to Your Community

Robert Frost said, "Good fences make good neighbors." So do good zoning laws and building-permit and inspection processes. As you begin to learn about the zoning in your community, you may begin to see that some zoning and building-permit processes actually work against efforts to provide affordable housing.

For example, most communities have worked to separate retail establishments from residential areas. The result has been the growth of suburbs and the disappearance of residences in downtown areas. When a new shopping mall is built out in the suburbs, shoppers have one less reason to be in the downtown core. Even small cities are seeing their cores become empty spaces instead of the thriving centers of activity they once were. My community is now actively promoting development of combined retail and residential properties in the downtown core.

> *We are the curators of life on earth.*
> HELEN CALDICOTT

You can get involved in the decisions that are made about your community. Serve on your neighborhood association, city planning committee, or city budget committee. You might even run for a seat on the city council.

As you learn the ins and outs of investing in rentals, you can help new rental owners work their way through the details. Become a member of your local rental-owner association. Serve on committees, especially those designed to help new rental owners.

Owning rental properties increases your investment in your community. You can use your position as a landowner to model behaviors you'd like to see emulated. And you can celebrate your success as a rental investor by giving back to your community as you increase your involvement in community activities. Your efforts will increase the intangible payoffs of your investment.

Summary

✔ Owning rental properties allows you to contribute to your community by offering safe, attractive, reasonably priced housing.

✔ Owning rental properties allows you to enhance you own sense of community.

✔ Owning rental properties lets you model progressive social and environmental practices.

✔ Owning rental properties lets you take an active role in protecting the planet.

✔ Owning rental properties allows you to live your values while you support yourself and your family.

■ *On the Internet*

To screen organizations with whom you do business according to working conditions and the locations of their factories, go to **www.coopamerica.org** Or try **www.responsibleshopper.org**

To check on the tax deductibility of your donations go to **www.itsdeductible.com**

If your investments are paying off so well you're ready to form your own charitable foundation, you'll find information for doing so at **www.programforgiving.org**

Another site for giving is **www.count-me-in.org**

Part Two

Getting
Ready

Chapter 4

Set Your Goals, Plot Your Strategy

Your Investment Plan

If it doesn't matter where you want to go, it doesn't matter which way you go.
THE CHESHIRE CAT TO ALICE

Without goals, Alice wandered around aimlessly, which may be okay for the hero of a children's fantasy but probably not what you want for your life. By the end of this chapter you should know where you want to go and have a good idea of how you are going to get there.

Your entire set of personal goals and objectives helps make you the person you are. While your investment strategies may seem to have little relationship to your goal to be a better parent or to learn to play the guitar, they are a part of your larger life goals. Your investment strategies need to be a part of the whole scheme and reflect your other more sublime goals, or those will be hard for you to attain.

If money looms large in your life, you can't go to bed until the checkbook balances, or you save all your cash register receipts and record your purchases every week, you will need different strategies than the person who just wanders like Alice and hopes things will come out even in the end.

In order to integrate your investment strategies with your larger life goals, you will need to consider your goals as a whole. As you read through this chapter and think about how you would like your life to progress in the next 10 or 20 years, look closely at the way your investments will reflect and affect those goals.

If you are like millions of Americans, one of your first financial goals may be to get your credit cards under control and reduce your consumer debt. You may have other financial issues you are concerned about. Before you proceed with setting goals and developing an investment plan, you need to know what your current financial picture looks like. It is time for you to develop your financial statement.

Your Financial Statement

Your financial statement is a snapshot—hopefully a candid photo— of your financial picture at a particular moment. From it you can see how your *assets*, what you own, compare to your *liabilities*, what you owe. The difference between the two is your *net worth*.

By preparing the statement in the categories shown below, you will also be able to compare assets that appreciate in value —such as real estate—with assets that depreciate in value—such as automobiles, boats, and big-screen television sets.

If you borrow money to purchase rental properties, your lender will require a financial statement. Doing one now will provide good practice, and it may reveal areas where you want to set some immediate financial goals. Many people are pleasantly surprised to realize how good their financial picture really is. Others find they need to consider some new spending habits.

Get Your Information Together Collect every scrap of paper that contains financial information—bank statements, mortgage information, all your bills, information about your money market accounts, CDs, all of it. Then, sort it into piles.

The first pile is for things you own, money you have in accounts and money that others owe you. Go around the house, garage, shop, and yard and write down an estimate of the value of your possessions. Don't worry about exact figures right now. You will refine these numbers later. Just try to get an accurate count of the valuables you own. Add the list of valuables you own to the list of money and paper valuables you own.

The second pile is for money you owe. Into this pile put your credit card bills, your home mortgage information, your rent and utility bills, your car or boat loans, and anything else on which you owe money.

List Your Assets From the pile of paper describing what you own, make a list of your cash balances in banks, credit unions, CDs, and money markets. Now list any notes receivable you hold. (By the way, that $500 you loaned your brother-in-law isn't an asset unless he signed a note.) Now list all your stocks and bonds and the surrender value of any life insurance. List your vested interest in any retirement funds and the value of all real estate you own. Finally, estimate the value of all vehicles and household and personal property you own. A sample financial statement is shown in the Appendix. You can use this as a check-list to make sure you haven't left out anything.

List Your Liabilities List what you owe to others from the second pile. List any notes payable. If you borrowed $500 from your brother-in-law without a note, don't list it. List bank loans and all credit card balances. Include your charge card at Penney's and your gas company charge cards, as well as your Visa and Master Cards.

List any loans on your car, furniture, boat, or any other item. Don't overlook installment payments on things like your health club membership and your student loans.

In this first effort your numbers will often be estimates. Don't take the time to include account numbers or to call for today's balance. Just remember that when you make a financial statement for the lender, you will need account numbers and addresses for all your creditors.

Now add up the value of everything on your asset list, and the total on your liability list. Then subtract your total liabilities from your total assets. The number you're left with is your *net worth*. I hope the number is a nice surprise for you.

Now you are ready to set your goals, with knowledge of your present financial picture firmly in your mind.

Set Your Goals

The exercise of setting goals and writing them down is a useful and enlightening experience. You will discover things about yourself you never knew consciously. You may find sudden clarity about your own values and the way they inform your goals. As the Danish poet Piet Hein said about tossing a coin to make a decision, "The moment the penny is in the air, you suddenly know what you're hoping."

In this goal-setting exercise, you will use a pattern to guide you. After you've gone through the exercise, you will have a short set of specific and immediate goals. You will also have a list of long-range goals. Because you will have learned the pattern, you will be able to update both sets of goals as your circumstances and viewpoint change.

Read through the exercise and think about each of the categories before you start writing. You may find you want to give yourself a day or two to ponder some of the items. Then write quickly, without pausing to think. This internal brainstorming will elicit your most honest responses. Remember, being honest with yourself is as important as it is difficult.

As in group brainstorming, write down everything that comes to your mind. Nothing is too far out, too ridiculous, or too expensive to be included. You will sort out goals by category and examine them more carefully later. You will also separate your goals by time line.

When you are ready to begin writing, find a place where you can be completely alone and undisturbed for at least an hour. Supply yourself with several sheets of paper and a pen, and try to avoid distractions during your brainstorming.

1. Describe what you want your life to look like in ten years. List all your goals, all the things you want to see, do, own, experience, visit, share, give, and receive in the next ten years. Be as wild and imaginative as you like, the more detail the better. You now have a list of goals.

2. Take three sheets of paper and label them, Year One, Year Five, and Year Ten. Now sort out the first list you made and transfer each goal to one of your sheets. Be realistic here. If one of your goals is to record a CD, remember that even if you start guitar lessons today, you might not be ready to cut a CD for at least five years. Or, if you buy a duplex tomorrow, the market may not improve enough for you to bid on Trump Tower by the end of the year.

3. You now have three lists of goals. Go through each list and select your top three to five priority goals. Describe each goal in as much detail as you can. What will it feel like, look like, smell like, taste like? The more you can visualize a goal, the more it means to you, and the more it will become a part of your world view.

Suppose you have long promised yourself you will learn to fly a plane. Visualize yourself on your first solo flight. What do you see from the cockpit? How does the plane smell? How does the rudder

Requirements for effective goals

1. Write goals down.
2. Describe goals in specific, measurable terms.
3. Visualize goals.
4. Make sure goals are achievable.
5. Set realistic deadlines for completing goals.
6. Break large goals down into manageable chunks.
7. Look for the potential problems that may keep you from reaching your goals.
8. Take action to remove or minimize potential problems.
9. Review your progress toward your goals on a regular basis.
10. Know what rewards you expect upon reaching a goal.

Adapted from *Executive Female*, July/Aug 1994.

feel in your hand? What does the instrument panel look like? What do you hear? The more you can imagine all your senses involved in achieving your goal, the more likely you are to stick to your dream.

When you finish this exercise, you should have a list of three to five goals for the next one-year, five-year, and ten-year time periods. Write the goals on an index card and put the card where you will see it daily. You may be surprised to find that in a month or two you seem to be nearing goals that seemed unreachable previously. I don't understand it, but it does work. And remember, *if it isn't written down, it isn't a goal, it's a dream.*

Many of your goals will need money, perhaps beyond what your salary might currently allow. I want to show you how investing in small rental properties will help you realize an income that will support your goals and dreams. In the rest of this chapter you'll learn how to develop a financial plan and investment strategies that will move you along the path to your goals.

Discover Your Financial Personality Type

Now that you have your financial goals in front of you, it's time to plan your strategy for reaching them. A critical piece of that plan will be your own financial personality. Are you a systematic planner and saver, or are you the impulsive sort who never has a dime left at the end of the month? Whatever type you are, it is possible to develop a plan that reflects your style and make it work to achieve your goals.

The non-profit Employee Benefit Research Institute has identified five financial personality types: Planners, Savers, Strugglers, Impulsives, and Deniers. No one of these types is consistently good at setting financial goals and working toward them. Neither is any type completely bad. Knowing your type will let you work around your bad habits and reinforce your better financial tendencies. Do you see your own financial tendencies in this list?

Planners   Twenty-three percent of us actually enjoy financial planning. Planners believe anyone can live well and retire well if they will just plan and save. Planners are willing to take reasonable risks if they believe it will increase their return.

Savers   The 19 percent who habitually save a portion of their income each month, the Savers, are seldom caught entirely off guard by unexpected financial events. Savers, however, are uncomfortable with risk. They save. They don't speculate in any form at any time. Savers will accumulate enough for a comfortable retirement, but their returns will never approach those of the Planners, who are willing to take some risk.

Strugglers   Those who are often caught by unexpected events and suffer financial setbacks are Strugglers. They represent about 18 percent of us, and although many maintain savings plans, they are easily deflected from their financial goals by the unexpected. Those of us with lower incomes often find ourselves among the Strugglers. We have less cushion to allow us to weather the unexpected.

Impulsives About 24 percent of Americans have good intentions but allow impulsive spending behaviors to sidetrack them. Impulsives are willing to take risks to reach their financial goals but may forget those goals in the heat of the moment, such as a really good sale. Since they lose sight of the goal, they are easily sidetracked, often suffer financial reversals, and give up on their goals.

Deniers The final 15 percent don't like financial planning in any shape or form. They may not believe that any effort on their part will improve their financial picture. Or they may feel that it is all beyond them and they are incapable of handling their own finances. Whatever the cause, Deniers will have the hardest time adjusting their attitudes and working out a financial plan. They will have to work hard to convince themselves that they can take control of their financial lives.

As you review the personality styles above, you will probably find yourself in one of the categories. You may see your style reflected in the financial statement you prepared. Consider your style as you work out your investment goals and design ways to accommodate or work around the weaknesses of your style. If you are an Impulsive, you may want to learn to leave your credit cards at home when you shop as a way to limit impulse spending. If you are a Saver, you may need to review the advantages of taking just a bit of risk as a way to improve your financial returns.

How Do You Feel About Risk? The way you define risk and your tolerance for risk depend on the habits and attitudes you developed growing up. Your previous experiences with investments and your present circumstances will color the way you view new investments.

Take the following Risk Tolerance Profile Test to see how those variables come together to produce your current attitude about financial risk. Check one answer for each question. Then use the scoring formula at the end to identify your tolerance for risk.

■ *Risk Tolerance Profile Test*

1. What word best describes your previous experience with investments?
   a. Terrible.
   b. About what I expected.
   c. Great.

2. When you were young, what did you do with the money you got, whether from jobs like babysitting, delivering papers, or your allowance?
   a. Saved most of it for something I really wanted.
   b. Spent some of it, saved some of it.
   c. Spent it almost as soon as I got it.

3. Where do you keep your savings — money you may need quickly?
   a. In a checking account at a bank or S & L.
   b. In a money market fund.
   c. Invested where it will be reasonably safe, but where it would earn higher interest than a traditional conservative investment pays.

4. What statement best describes your attitude toward money when you were in college?
   a. I worked part time to help pay my expenses.
   b. I counted on my parents, scholarships, and student loans to cover my expenses.
   c. I counted on my parents and didn't worry much about how the bills would be paid.

5. You've just won $100,000 in a lottery. Where would you invest it?
   a. Certificates of deposit (CDs).
   b. Long-term U.S. Government bonds.
   c. An independent movie being produced by a friend.

6. When you were growing up, how did your parents view borrowing money?
   a. Their only loan was the mortgage on the house.
   b. They bought consumer products—cars and appliances on credit.
   c. They had credit card debt that caused financial problems for the family.

7. Which of the following statements best describes your behavior at work?
   a. I almost never express my ideas or opinions. I do not want to rock the boat.
   b. I occasionally express my ideas or opinions.
   c. I always express my ideas and opinions. I believe diverse opinions stimulate creativity.

8. A $20,000 investment that you made six months ago has increased in value by 20%. What action do you take?
   a. Sell your shares and take the profits.
   b. Stay with the investment. It may continue to increase in value.
   c. Buy more shares. Their value will probably increase even more.

9. You've known since you filed your federal income tax return, two months ago, that you will receive a $5,000 refund. Today, it finally arrived. What do you do with the money?
   a. Pay off $5,000 of your credit card debt.
   b. Use it as part of a down payment on a duplex as part of your long-term investment program.
   c. Spend it on the big-screen TV you've wanted for years.

10. How many years before you plan to leave your job, for retirement or for other opportunities?
    a. 5 years.
    b. 10 to 15 years.
    c. 20 or more years.

To score your Risk Tolerance Profile: Give yourself one point for all *a* answers, two points for all *b* answers, and three points for all *c* answers.

If you scored from 10 to 16, you are a conservative investor, from 17 to 22 you have an average tolerance for risk, and from 23 to 30 you have a high tolerance for risk. Remember, these numbers merely reflect your preferred approach to investing. They are not value judgments.

Now you know how you stack up compared to the rest of the investment world in your tolerance for risk. Keep your risk tolerance in mind as you begin to develop your long-term investment plan.

Your Financial Plan: The Big Picture

As you start work on your plan, remember that you will learn about investing as you go along. Don't expect to "make a killing," on your first—or second—purchase. The TV gurus who tell you, for example, to rush out and find distressed properties and make your fortune are trying to sell you something, usually books and seminars. They are not particularly interested in your success, or even your survival. A good plan, with realistic time lines, will be your best guide to financial independence.

Remember also, that your plan should fit your circumstances. If you are still employed, you might be able to consider large loans and short financing periods. You may have enough income to balance a small or negative cash flow. After you retire, however, you'll probably want as much cash flow as possible, and that means smaller loans, for longer periods.

Many lenders will insist on knowing the maximum amount you have available to you on any lines of credit. You can see why. If you suddenly run up that $25,000 line of credit, your financial picture changes significantly.

Your financial plan should consist of two parts: a general statement of your financial goals, and a specific plan that includes time lines and dollar figures. Obviously, both dollar figures and time frames will be your best estimates. Numbers will give you a standard to shoot for, however, and you will refine both as time goes by.

For the general, big-picture plan, consider the personal goals you formulated. Rewrite those goals now in financial terms. This is hard work. Suppose your plan includes college expenses for the kids.

Call two or three colleges and find out what tuition, room and board, and books and supplies cost on average for a year. Or find those costs on the Internet or at your public library. Add some percentage for inflation, depending on how long it will be before your children are ready for college. Put the result into your financial plan.

Is one of your goals to retire at a certain age? Will you retire to travel, or will you take early retirement in order to start that business you've always dreamed of? Can you depend on the income from a new business? How much will you need to live on after you retire? Attach your best guesses for times and dollar figures for these goals.

Be as specific as you can be about the times and income needed for your goals. If you've promised yourself a new Mercedes, find out how much that new Mercedes will cost and add some percentage for the number of years before you will be in the market for a new car. You'll find some examples of financial plans and investment goals farther along in this chapter. Notice that they all have dollar amounts attached.

Work down through your top five to ten goals this way. Attach general estimates of both cost and time to each goal. When you have outlined your financial plan, you are ready to fill in the details.

Your Financial Plan: The Details

As you develop your plan, you need to focus on three specifics that will drive many of your investment decisions: the amount of cash you need on a steady basis, your need to take chunks of cash out of your investments periodically, and your net worth goal.

Increase Current Cash Flow Your need for cash depends on your goals and circumstances. If you are a well-paid, thirty-five-year-old, you may devise a plan that pushes cash flow well into the future. If however, you have ten years or fewer to retirement, or until you need cash for college expenses, increased cash flow may be an immediate goal. You would develop different financial plans for these different scenarios. Regardless of where events occur on your time line, you need to plan for a long-term, fairly steady flow of cash into your checking account, occasional large chunks of cash, or some combination of these.

The way you craft your transactions when you buy or sell rentals will be a function of your cash needs. Before you make an offer, you need to figure out how to balance your down payment with debt service and costs, in order to yield the cash you need. In each chapter that deals with buying and selling, I'll remind you to review your goals and to base your investment strategy on those goals.

Periodic Cash Withdrawals Look back at your goals. When are you planning to need large chunks of cash? Whether it's for your daughter's tuition or your parents' Golden Wedding Anniversary cruise, put your need for cash in your plan and attach a dollar amount.

From the example of Caitlin's Financial Plan below, you can see that she has several options for getting money out of her investment. Any of these could work for you depending on your circumstances. If you

> *It's not how much you make, it's how much you keep, and how many generations you keep it.*
> ROBERT KIYOSAKI

can predict your need for large cash withdrawals at specific times, put that in your plan. I'll suggest some strategies for getting chunks of cash out of your rentals in Chapter 11.

Build Your Net Worth Establishing a net worth goal gives you something concrete to aim for and something to measure, and watching your net worth grow is extremely satisfying. Even when you have just replaced the third water heater in one month, you can tell yourself that it may have been a trying month, but your equity and your net worth are still increasing.

As your net worth increases, so does your borrowing power. For example, I recently refinanced a property as a way to lower my mortgage payments and take cash out for some improvements. My equity in the property, hence my net worth, had increased enough that the lender accepted the property tax assessment as the value of the property, which saved me the several thousand dollars a new appraisal would have cost.

Caitlin's Financial Plan   Like many of us, Caitlin had more credit card debt than was prudent, she kept poor records, and she didn't budget. When she suddenly inherited $100,000, she realized she needed to reorder her financial priorities and to manage that money responsibly. Caitlin did her plan in two steps: a general life style plan first, then a concrete investment plan using her inheritance as the foundation.

■ *Caitlin's Financial Goals*

Action	Time Line
1. Change daily spending habits as a way to generate cash (see Chapter 9)	immediately
2. Consolidate credit card debt to one card and check out credit unions for cards and financial help	2 months
3. Locate duplex to buy and make offer ($50/month/unit cash flow)	9 months
4. Find and purchase second property	3 years
5. Refinance one property per year for family travel	5 through 9 years
6. Retire early on cash from rentals	10 years

■ Caitlin's Detailed Investment Plan

Projected Performance of Each Duplex in First Five Years

Year	Market value	Appreciation in mrkt value	Loan payoff	Total equity	Tax saving	Cash flow
0	$100,000	$ 0	$ 0	$25,000	$ 0	$ 0
1	105,000	5,000	1,524	31,524	650	1,350
2	110,250	10,250	3,125	38,375	650	1,350
3	115,760	15,760	4,775	45,535	650	1,350
4	121,550	21,550	6,475	53,025	650	1,350
5	127,630	27,630	8,225	60,855	650	1,350

This table reflects Caitlin's hopes and strategies. It is an investment plan, not a report or statement. When developing the plan Caitlin assumed that the market would improve at about five percent a year—a conservative assumption. You may remember from Chapter 2 that she actually experienced a seven percent increase in market value. She further assumed that her rents and her expenses, hence her cash flow, would not change over the five-year period.

From the table, you can see that Caitlin hopes to realize $6,735 in total cash flow per duplex in five years, and to have amassed equity of about $60,000 in each duplex by the end of five years. She will also have enjoyed a total of $3,250 in tax savings per duplex over five years.

Based on her assumptions, Caitlin can project the return she will enjoy on her investment and can even calculate the value of a new property she might be able to afford at the end of five years. Let's look at her return on investment (ROI) first.

If, at the end of the first year, Caitlin calculated her return on her investment of $25,000, she would add her cash flow, loan reduction equity, appreciation equity, and tax savings, then divide that total by her down payment, and multiply the result by 100.

■ *Comparison of Total Equity After Year 1 and Year 5*

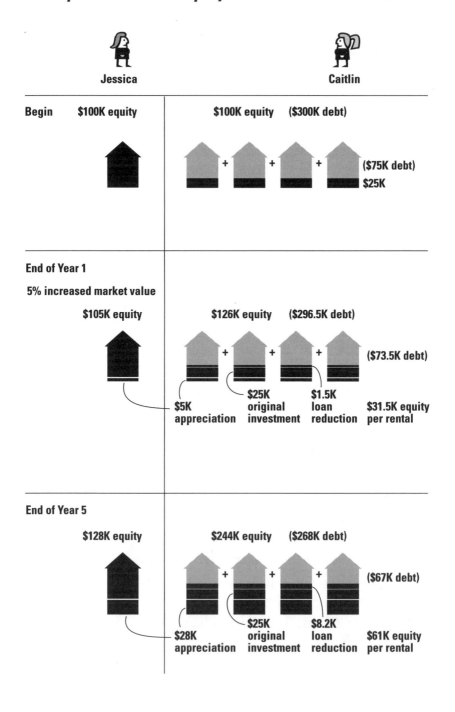

Jessica   Caitlin

Begin $100K equity   **$100K equity   ($300K debt)**

($75K debt)
$25K

End of Year 1

5% increased market value

$105K equity   **$126K equity   ($296.5K debt)**

($73.5K debt)

$5K $25K $1.5K
appreciation original   loan $31.5K equity
             investment   reduction   per rental

End of Year 5

$128K equity   **$244K equity   ($268K debt)**

($67K debt)

$28K $25K $8.2K
appreciation original   loan $61K equity
             investment   reduction   per rental

Caitlin's calculations look like this:

cash flow	$1,347
loan reduction	1,524
appreciation	5,000
tax saving	650
total	$8,521

$$\frac{\$8,521 \text{ return}}{\$25,000 \text{ down payment}} = 0.341 \times 100 = 34.1\% \text{ return}$$

Caitlin's return of 34.1% is considerably better than she would have had in the stock market, which is what she is after.

Many investors in real estate also calculate a return on equity every year, because they plan to dispose of a property when their return falls below some pre-determined value. Their investment plans often call for frequent sale and purchase of properties, a much more aggressive investment plan than Caitlin is using.

Caitlin planned to sell one or more of her properties and buy a larger complex as soon as she could afford to do so. She had hoped to be able to do that in five years. To calculate how much she could afford to pay for a new property, based on the returns from just one of her four rentals, Caitlin used the formula:

$$\frac{\text{equity available to invest}}{\% \text{ down payment required}} = \text{new property cost}$$

At the end of five years Caitlin expects to have about $61,000 available to invest in a new property. If she expects to pay 25 percent down, she can buy a $243,620 property.

$$\frac{\text{total equity} = \$61,000}{0.25 \text{ down payment}} = \$243,620$$

If she buys another four-plex and can pay just 10 percent down, she could purchase a $610,000 property.

$$\frac{\$61,000}{0.10} = \$610,000$$

The rental and sales markets may not allow Caitlin, or you, to follow your investment plan exactly. However, your plan will let you to play "what if" and try out various possibilities. And because your plan will be lodged in your subconscious, your financial decisions will begin to reflect your plan and enhance your investment career.

By now you should know a lot more about your current financial picture. And you've thought long and hard about what you would like it to look like next year and in the years to come. Your financial plan has numbers in it, both for time targets and for financial goals. Obviously you can't predict either money or time with precision. But writing down concrete goals lets you do two things. First, you have something to shoot for and to measure your progress against. Second, you can work backward from a target date and financial goal to see just what actions you will need to take to accomplish a goal on time. *Write it down, commit to making it happen, and figure out how you are going to do it.*

Review Your Plan Every few months, sit down with your spouse or partner and review your plan. Adjust your goals as they change. Keep track of your progress and the increase in the value of your real estate portfolio and your net worth. Congratulate yourself on your accomplishments and celebrate your successes.

Summary

✔ Develop your financial statement as a way to understand your current financial position. You may get a pleasant surprise.

✔ Identify your investment style, then learn to work around the weak points of your style and emphasize the strong points.

✔ Write down your financial goals in as much detail as you can. Review your goals frequently. The more you think about your goals, the more chance you have of attaining them.

✔ Remember that the details include numbers. Use one of the online retirement estimate calculators to figure out what you may need at retirement, then plug that figure into your goals statement.

✔ Your plan is a working document. Review it frequently and adjust it as needed.

■ *On the Internet*

These sites provide calculators and worksheets that allow you to figure out how much income you will need in retirement. Use them to provide dollar figures for your investment plan:

The Quicken.com Retirement Planner is at
www.quicken.com/retirement/planner

The T. Rowe Price calculator lets you try some "what if" scenarios at **www.troweprice.com/retincome/IC**

The AARP calculator is at **www.aarp.org/bulletin**

The American Savings Education Council's site offers a Financial Facts Tool Kit. Phone (800) 732-0330, or order a copy at
www.sec.gov/investor/pubs/toolkit.htm

Other government retirement calculators are at
www.choosetosave.org/tools/fincalcs.htm

Chapter Five

Identify
Your Team:
Many Heads Are
Better Than One

Companies have a board of directors.
You should have one too.
ROBERT KIYOSAKI.

If two heads are better than one, then six should make a winning team. Buying, renting, and selling property is a complex activity. You need access to lots of information if you're going to make good decisions and avoid pitfalls. Unless you have unlimited time and soak up information like a sponge, you should plan to rely on the advice of a team of professionals, at least in the early stages of your venture.

Pick Your Team Members

My investment team includes an attorney, a tax and accounting advisor, two Realtors, an insurance agent, and a property manager. The information and support they give me reduce stress, increase the time I have for other things, and increase my profits.

Attorney Sometimes I think I know a fair amount about the legal aspects of rental ownership. Then I talk to my attorney, and she brings up an issue I hadn't thought of. Because this happens so often, I consult her on every major transaction and I schedule twice-a-year appointments just to update her on my activities.

This many appointments with an attorney can be expensive, but I rarely spend more than 30 minutes on these check-ups. Given the potential cost of cleaning up some problem I've blundered into through ignorance, I consider our little chats to be good insurance.

Tax Preparer and Accountant The tax code covering income property was complicated even before the tax simplification measure of 1986 rewrote nearly all of it. Now the code is so complex, it is all but impossible to understand. It also changes yearly. I have no desire, and no ability, to keep up with the changes.

Like your attorney, a good tax advisor will save you money, sometimes in ways you had not anticipated. For example, if your return is audited, your tax preparer will encourage you to let her attend the audit in your place. This isn't just her generous nature at work. Having your tax preparer represent you at an audit limits the topics the auditor can address. Further, if you have found a tax preparer who seldom loses money in an audit, the local IRS officials may begin to do cursory audits of her clients or to avoid her returns altogether.

You need to be aware that tax advisors and accountants can have very different perspectives. A good accountant makes sure your financial information is accurate. A good tax preparer makes sure you are paying the minimum tax required by law. The questions you ask in interviewing tax consultants and/or accountants will help you determine their focus.

Your accountant will help you set up record-keeping processes that make keeping track of your investments easy and support the needs of your tax preparer. My tax preparer and my accounting advisor are one and the same, an arrangement that makes the advice I get consistent.

Real Estate Agent In the beginning you need to have the help of a real estate licensee both to buy and to sell property. You need advice and help when you're looking for a property and when you're ready buy. And you'll want someone out there hustling for you when you're ready to sell.

You can, of course, deal directly with a seller or a buyer and draw up your own documents. However, many a first-time buyer didn't think to ask if the sump pump worked or just assumed the new side-by-side fridge or beautiful flowering shrubs came with the property. For the first couple of transactions, you really need someone coaching you through the details.

One Realtor can help you both in buying and selling property, but two Realtors with separate focuses are often better. The legal and *fiduciary*, or monetary, relationships a Realtor has with a buyer are very different from those she has with a seller. When you are buying a property, the Realtor who shows you the property and helps you make an offer is usually working for the seller. As a matter of fact, the *listing* Realtor and the seller have a signed contract specifying the terms under which the seller has *employed* the Realtor. The Realtor showing you the property is usually, legally, the employee of the seller.

Regardless of how you feel about the listing Realtor who shows you properties, and regardless of the amount of time you've spent together, she is required by law to put the interest of the seller ahead of your interest as buyer. As you can see, you may want your own advisor. When you're buying, that person is called a *buyer's agent*.

My Realtor recently told me she is reluctant to begin helping a new buyer find a property before she has a signed agreement showing her as the buyer's agent. She has too often had the experience of spending many hours showing prospective buyers property after property, only to have them find something on their own, and then buy it from another Realtor without a word to her.

You can see how unfair it is to cut the person who has invested time and effort on your behalf out of the deal. Especially when you are an investor, you are looking for a team member with whom you may have a life-long relationship. You want your Realtor on *your* team.

Consider signing a six-month buyer's-agent agreement at first. This will be an important relationship for both of you, and you want to make sure you are compatible. Once you have developed a track record, you may forgo contracts since your Realtor knows she will be paid, and you know you can count on her to protect your interests.

In many states, Realtors specializing in *residential* properties are licensed under different terms than those specializing in *commercial* properties. Commercial Realtors are seldom members of multiple-listing organizations, with whom you would expect to find duplexes and four-plexes listed.

Because federal programs such as FHA define residential properties as those with one to four units, most state real estate licensing regulations use the same definitions. If you are buying or selling one to four units, you will need the services of a Realtor who specializes in residential properties. Buying or selling five or more units will require the services of a commercial Realtor.

I have a commercial Realtor and a residential Realtor, because my commercial Realtor doesn't usually deal with smaller complexes, and he doesn't belong to the local multiple listing association. If I want to buy or sell a duplex or four-plex, I need to consult my residential Realtor.

I don't use a buyer's-agent agreement because I've come to trust my commercial and residential Realtors, and they trust me. I've worked with them long enough to know them well, and because they both own rentals, we think along the same lines. You, too, may find it useful to seek out Realtors who own rentals, since their perspectives may be closer to yours.

Property Managers When I began my real estate adventure, I couldn't imagine paying someone else to manage a couple of rentals. How much work could it be, after all? As it turned out, it wasn't property management that caused me stress, it was tenant management.

Because management organizations handle a sizeable number of properties, they often know how to set rents and manage tenants better than owners. My managers have an excellent reputation, so new renters seek them out. The staff is meticulous about tenant screening, which saves me money. And they are always available to answer my questions and work with my remodeling projects. I would need to spend more than 40 hours a week managing my properties, and I'm quite sure I wouldn't do the professional job they do. I think I get more than my money's worth.

Insurance Agent As you begin to develop your long-range financial goals, you need to plan for the protection of your assets. In the beginning of your rental ownership adventure, your insurance agent should advise you about hazard insurance for your properties, liability insurance to protect your assets, and personal policies such as life insurance and long-term-care insurance.

You will want to establish a *liability umbrella insurance policy* early in your investment efforts, and should have your liability policy in place when you buy your first rental. Coverage and cost of all kinds of insurance differ widely. Shop around for the best deals. Ask your financial advisor to discuss the sort of coverage you want and to find plans for you to review.

Your lender will require you to carry hazard insurance on your rental. You will have to bring an *insurance binder*—a written promise to insure the property—to closing and pay for the policy at closing. Your insurance agent will help you navigate through the thicket of coverage and policy provisions and help you balance premium cost and deductibles to fit your circumstances.

Getting Your Team Together

You now have a list of team positions. How do you fill them? The process for locating each consultant may differ depending on the position, but in all cases you'll want to have a list of questions to ask prospective team members. Asking friends for referrals is useful only if your friends have similar personal and financial issues.

Finding Your Attorney   One way to find an attorney is to call your local bar association; you'll find it in the yellow pages. The people at the bar association can tell you which lawyers include real estate in their specialties. They will also be able to tell you who is taking new clients, but they will not make recommendations. You will still need to use interviews or a trial period to determine if you and a potential attorney are a good match.

My long-time attorney just happens to specialize in real estate. But if you already have an attorney, you may find that real estate is not one of his areas of expertise. However, he will be able to recommend several names. A referral from your attorney has a couple of advantages. He will recommend attorneys he thinks will be compatible with your style, and the attorneys he recommends may be more willing to take you on as a new client if you are a referral.

Questions to Ask a Prospective Attorney:
1. Is real estate one of your specialties?
2. How much experience do you have advising real estate investors?
3. Will you review my financial plan with me and alert me to steps I'll need to take to protect my assets?
4. How much experience do you have drafting contracts for real estate sales? I may be either a buyer or a seller at various times in my investment career.
5. Are you available for a long-term legal relationship?
6. What is your fee structure?
7. Do you offer an initial free consultation?

Your job in the relationship is to be as honest as possible about your financial plans and circumstances, and to inform your attorney of changes in your financial status.

Finding Your Tax Preparer For tax preparation and accounting advice, you may find one person who does both, as I have. Or you may want to interview several people for separate positions. The focus and goals of the person you select should be similar to yours. For example, I want a tax preparer who is dedicated to keeping me from paying any more taxes than absolutely necessary. This is not tax evasion. It is tax avoidance, and it is completely legal and important to your long-term investment goals.

For the first property I sold, I consulted a CPA for help on the taxes. I sold the property on a contract, what the IRS calls an installment sale, and the tax issues were beyond me. When the CPA finished her calculations, she showed me the $15,000 tax bill and said with a smile, "Well, that's a nice profit, Mabel." In spite of my choking and gasping at the bite the IRS was going to take out of my "nice profit," she simply couldn't hear me say, "Isn't there some way to reduce that tax bill?"

If I were looking again, I would talk to my friends about their experiences with tax preparers, and I would ask my attorney for referrals. I would also get some names from the yellow pages to interview, focusing on people associated with bookkeeping services. They seem to be especially sensitive to bottom-line issues.

Questions to Ask a Prospective Tax Preparer:
1. How many years have you been in business?
2. How long will you keep my returns? Will you fax copies to lenders at my request?
3. How much audit experience do you have? Will you represent me at audits?

4. How do you charge for tax preparation? What do you charge for preparation? What do you charge for tax planning and consulting?

5. Can we meet to discuss tax-reduction strategies for me early in the tax year?

6. Are you available to answer questions by phone?

7. Do you have experience with tax issues involved with 1031 real estate exchanges?

8. May I see a copy of the tax-preparation package you send your clients?

Your job with regard to your tax preparer is to keep her fully informed of your buy and sell plans and transactions. Let her know early if you plan to make a change that could affect your tax status. And, of course, try to keep your records in order so that you can discuss them off an on throughout the tax year.

Finding Your Realtor While friends may be a good source of referrals for some of the other professionals, they are not the first people you want to ask about Realtors. Most of your friends will have bought personal residences, an experience far different from the one you'll face as an investor. The skills and attitudes required of the Realtor who works with rental properties are different from those needed by the person who works with single-family, owner-occupied homes, and the help you'll need as an investor is also different.

You can develop a list of names from for-sale ads of rental properties in the newspaper. If Realtors marketing rentals hold open houses, make a point of going and meeting the Realtor. Don't identify yourself as looking for a Realtor. Pay attention to the way the Realtor interacts, thinking you are a potential buyer. If your experience is positive, make an appointment to discuss your needs at some later time.

Once you have located a couple of likely candidates, you're ready to interview for your buyer's agent. You can negotiate with any Realtor to represent you as a buyer's agent. You may, of course, have to pay your agent, depending on the transaction. But you should be able to negotiate terms you can both live with, and she may save you more money than she costs. She should also be able to expect that she will get the listing when you get ready to sell one of your properties.

Questions to Ask a Prospective Buyer's Agent.

(from *The Associated Press* August 1994)

1. Will you always be loyal to me?
2. Will you negotiate only for me?
3. Will you show me properties that fit my financial goals?
4. Will you keep confidential my financial information, negotiating strategies, and goals?
5. Will you conduct a comparable market analysis to help determine a property's true value?
6. Will you research seller information, e.g. true rents and true operating expenses, to help in negotiations?
7. Will you research the seller's motives for selling?
8. Will you keep confidential my motives for buying?
9. Will you investigate the property's weaknesses and work for full disclosure?

Your job, vis a vis your Realtor(s), is to make your desires clear. Do your homework so you can be specific about your goals. For example, "I want a two- to four-family rental in one of these three neighborhoods. I can spend about this much money and I can schedule a half day each week to look at properties." Show her the real-estate ads you've clipped. Be prepared to make decisions as fast as you can. Your Realtor's time is the primary thing she has to sell.

Finding Your Property Manager

I learned about selecting property managers the hard way—I had to fire my first two. With the first there was disagreement on fundamental management philosophy. She rented a single-family home to six college football players, who hung a dart board on the dining room wall. Unfortunately for me, their aim was really bad. They were even worse furniture movers than they were dart players. By the time they left, they had torn up the hardwood floors, damaged the vinyl in the kitchen, and, of course, ruined the dining room wall.

Worse yet, because she felt sorry for the "guys," the manager had not collected enough deposit to pay for the damages. It was a short, unhappy relationship.

My second manager insisted on working on a cash-only basis. She wouldn't produce invoices for goods or services or monthly statements. That should have been my first clue, but I was new in the business and far too trusting. I fired her when she refused to give me written accounts of rents received and expenses paid. I've learned to be suspicious of people who don't want to account for financial dealings in writing.

In order to find a competent manager who fits your style, you may have to interview several candidates. Before you even talk to a potential manager, do your homework. Get the addresses of several properties managed by each of your candidates. You can find these in the rental ads in the newspaper.

Drive by the properties. Do they need paint? Are the yards kept up? Are junker cars parked about? Cruise through about 9 p.m. to check out the noise level. If there is a resident manager, stop in and talk a minute. Then interview a couple of tenants. Ask them how quickly repairs are made and how rapid the response is to emergencies. Ask if they like living there.

You may feel more like a renter than a property investor, because at this point you are trying to look at the property through tenants' eyes. If your tenants are not satisfied with the management, they will not stay. Long-term tenants are valuable, and you want a management firm that is committed to keeping good tenants happy. Your research will help you narrow down your candidate list to a couple of managers you will want to talk to.

Questions to Ask a Prospective Property Manager:

1. Do you have references I can contact?
2. May I see a copy of the monthly and year-end financial statements that you send your clients?
3. How many evictions did you process last year?
4. Describe your maintenance philosophy. Are your maintenance people employees or are they independent contractors? If they are independent contractors, are they all licensed and bonded?
5. What was the turnover rate in your office last year?
6. What was the average length of time a unit stayed vacant last year? What is your vacancy rate now?
7. How often do you inspect occupied units? How often does someone do a drive-by inspection of the exteriors?
8. May I have copies of these documents to review: the contract I will sign with you, your rental agreement, and the move-in/move-out condition checklist?

Finding Your Insurance Agent The way an insurance office handles claims for auto accidents and damage due to leaky pipes will be a good guide to the service you can expect when you have a claim. Ask your friends and co-workers who they like and why. Ask both about the company and about specific agents.

Questions to Ask a Prospective Insurance Agent:

1. How much will I save in premiums if you carry all my insurance—auto, homeowners, personal liability, etc?
2. What is your average time for claim processing?
3. How large is your office? Will there always be someone available to help me during business hours?
4. Do real people answer your office telephone?
5. How often do you plan to review my coverage with me?
6. How often will you inspect my properties for appropriateness of coverage?

Finally, an important question to ask all advisors: Do you return phone calls promptly? Accessibility is critical. If you need advice and can't find your advisor, it's just like not having one.

Paying for Advice

By this point you may be wondering how you're going to pay for all this advice. Usually, professional advice is a bit like electricity; you only pay for the time you use. Until you own several million dollars worth of real estate, you will not pay retainers to accountants or lawyers. The only person who may be on your monthly payroll is the property manager.

Many professionals offer a 30-minute introductory appointment for no charge. Be sure to ask if a free get-acquainted time is available when you call. You may be able to make the choice for or against a team member based on this brief conversation and save yourself some time and money.

It is hard to assess the value of advice that saves you money and keeps you out of trouble. With your tax person, you can analyze your returns and estimate fairly closely what her tax advice is worth. I estimate that my tax person saves me two to three dollars for every dollar I spend. For legal and accounting advice the analysis is trickier.

I suggest you set up your team and give it a year. Then look carefully at your bills; tax time is a good time to do this. Think about the advice you've received. Try to estimate both the amount of money and the amount of time you have saved by having professional advice, and remember, the cost of professional advice is tax deductible.

Investing successfully in real estate is a complex venture. Few people try to learn all the facets of the process, let alone keep abreast of the changes, by themselves. Your team of legal and financial advisors will supply advice and guidance as you develop your investments.

Summary

✔ Identify your professional advisors before you need their advice.

✔ Interview potential advisors. This will be a long-term relationship.

✔ Be prepared to hold up your end of the relationship. Do your homework. Be prepared for appointments. Keep your records in order.

✔ Many fees are negotiable; be sure you ask.

✔ Don't pay for advice you don't intend to follow.

■ On the Internet

To learn about the various Realtor designations go to **www.nationalassociationofRealtors.com**

To find a Realtor in your area, try these sites:
www.prudential.com
www.remax.com
www.century21.com

To find an insurance agent go to **www.Insure.com**

Chapter Six

Learn *the* Ropes:
Real Estate Investing 101

One must learn by doing the thing; for though you think you know it, you have no certainty until you try.
SOPHOCLES

As Chapter 1 makes clear, you don't need to know everything about real estate to invest successfully in rental properties. The things you *do* need to know, you can learn in small pieces as you go along. This chapter will help you start that process.

One challenge is that the few things you do need to know, you need to know all at the same time. It would be nice to be able to just turn to the appropriate chapter and read it the night before you need the information. Unfortunately, reading is a linear process—we read sentence by sentence. Buying a property is a process that looks more like an octopus—it spreads out in all directions.

When approaching your first purchase, you'll need to be simultaneously learning about your local sales and rental markets, doing your homework to compare properties, considering the contingencies you want to write into your first offer to purchase, and lining up your financing. All these activities sound intimidating, but if you skimmed the first couple of chapters, you probably discovered you already know a great deal. This chapter will help you fill in the gaps. As the title, Real Estate Investing 101, suggests, it is an introduction to the topic. Reading this book will be just the beginning of a life-long education in real estate. You will have to keep learning about your market. What was true about the market in June is not true by December.

To get started, you need to learn about three things: your local rental market, your real estate sales market, and some of the jargon of the industry.

Your Local Rental Market

When I say you need to know about your market, I don't mean you should be able to quote, off the top of your head, the high and low rents for a one-bedroom apartment this week. You should, however, know both what the general range of rents is for units in various parts of town, and what the current trend is. Is the market in each area going up, going down, or staying flat? You need to be a trend spotter.

How do you learn about the rental market? Fortunately, you can do some of your initial homework sitting on your deck, with your feet up, and a cup of coffee in your hand. Your first source for rental information is your local newspaper. Read the rentals-available section weekly; most rental ads appear in weekend editions. Property owners with rentals to let communicate with prospective renters through the newspaper. You should be eavesdropping on that conversation.

After you've studied a couple of weekend papers, you will begin to develop a sense of what your market is doing. Signs of market stagnation include ads offering *first month free, no deposits, move-in specials, and summer rates!* The more of these phrases you see in the ads, the more depressed your local rental market may be. Signs of a hot rental market include ads specifying *no pets, no Section 8, and one-year lease.*

The market drives rents and the conditions of renting—leases, deposits, pet restrictions. When there are more renters than vacancies, property owners can be selective. They impose high rents, high deposits, and other conditions that allow them to increase their profits. When the market is soft, landowners may be virtually paying renters to sign up or to stay longer. A vacancy rate above five percent is considered a good market for renters, but a poor market for property owners. A market with less than five percent vacancies is considered a tight market for renters, and a good one for rental owners.

When you are ready to compare rents and amenities among the kind of units you're interested in, it is time to go directly to the sources by attending rental open houses and calling the phone numbers listed in rental ads. You can make phone calls from home, just as you can read the newspaper on the deck. Call the number listed in an ad and ask the questions you would ask if you were a prospective renter:

- How big is the unit ?
- What appliances are included?
- What utilities are included in the rent?

Type up a list of questions before you call and make multiple copies of it. Then fill in the information on each unit you call about. This way you will collect all the pertinent information on each unit.

More and more, landowners and management agencies hold open houses to solicit tenants, especially in soft markets. They often provide a flyer containing the information you want. If your questions are not answered by a flyer, you have the list you prepared for your telephone research, so you are primed with questions.

You want to be a trend spotter. You need to develop a sense of how rents change according to the size of the units, the amenities, and location. Do property owners in your area normally pay all utilities, or just water, sewer, and garbage? Is it the norm in your area for renters to pay for their own cable service, even in larger complexes? What are the usual deposits, refundable and non-refundable? Do most rentals accept pets or not? Do most land-owners require a year-long lease, or are rents month-to-month? You may choose to place your own rentals outside the mainstream with regard to some of the trends. But you need to know where the mainstream is, so you can calculate your risk in adopting practices that are not standard for your area.

If you have never gone shopping for an apartment to rent, telephoning and visiting advertised units will be an education. Not only will you develop your financial knowledge, you will begin seeing the breadth of the market. You will see units you wouldn't live in if the owner paid you, you will see units you couldn't afford to rent at twice your income, and you'll see everything in between. It will be eye-opening, and it should be great fun.

Your Local Sales Market

After you've surveyed the market for rental units available in your area, you're ready to take a look at rentals that are for sale. You may have established some idea of the sort of unit you can afford and would enjoy owning just by driving around or visiting open houses. Now you are ready to check out prices on properties you'd like to own.

Rental complexes of more than six units seldom show up in the for-sale section of newspapers. Commercial brokers cultivate life-long relationships with the people who buy, hold, and sell these properties. Before a broker advertises such a property, she will have called everyone on her list to see if a current client is interested— another reason to develop a relationship with at least one commercial broker.

Rental properties of one to four units are often advertised in newspapers and real estate sales booklets. You should be reading all the brochures you can find. A good way to educate yourself about your local sales market for these properties is to prepare a table with your targeted neighborhoods across the top and listings from newspapers and brochures down the side. Newspapers often list the address of the property for sale; brochures may have either addresses or MLS (Multiple Listing Service) numbers. Enter information from each Saturday and Sunday newspaper and from all the real estate brochures you've gathered.

By the time you have accumulated four weeks of information, you will know more about the prices of units in your target areas than most real estate agents in town. You will also have learned what the range of listing prices is, whether prices are changing and in what direction, how fast rental properties are selling, and which neighborhoods you can afford to buy into.

Attend open houses for rental units that are for sale. Many mortgage companies provide information sheets at open houses describing the interest rates and terms they are prepared to offer to qualified buyers. If a loan officer is present at the open house, introduce yourself and say you are starting to think about investing in rentals. Find out what kinds of financing the lender he represents has available. Open houses are good places to make contacts and expand your network.

> If your local market is depressed, you may be able to find some good deals on rentals for sale. However, you will want to structure your purchase to be consistent with increased vacancies and lower rents. This may be a time to make a larger down payment so your mortgage payments will be smaller. With smaller payments, decreased rents and increased vacancies will be of less concern to you. As a prudent investor, you will want to be ready to buy when the market is depressed, not when it is sky high.

See if you can answer these questions using the table you've created:

- What do the various configurations—two units, four units, or larger—sell for in your target locations?
- How do prices for older buildings compare to prices for newer buildings?
- How do the conditions and amenities compare?
- What kind of financing is customary in your area?
- What is the current trend—have prices been going up or down in the past six months?
- Can you make any educated guesses about how the trend will continue, and for how long?

The list of questions you will want to answer is much longer, and will be developed in Chapter 7. For now, you are primarily interested in gaining a sense of your local market, so you will be prepared to focus on a few properties to analyze in detail before you are ready to purchase.

Continuing Education

The more involved and interested you become in owning rental properties, the more you will want to learn how to maximize your return and increase your enjoyment in your investments. Be selective about where you go to learn more about rental investments.

As we saw from the corporate scandals of 2002, there seems to be a tendency for people to try to find shortcuts to wealth. Many radio and television gurus and seminar providers capitalize on that tendency. To protect yourself from these twenty-first century snake-oil salesmen, remember that few real shortcuts are both effective and ethical. Your goals and financial circumstances are different from the next investor's. Each market is different, and each person will use different strategies for investing in rentals. By studying your local market, you will know more than the seminar salesman who is touting the latest formula for making millions in real estate.

Classes at community colleges and junior colleges are a different matter. Both credit classes and community education classes can provide you with basic skills to analyze properties, calculate returns and tax consequences, and give you the confidence you need to begin your investment activities. The classes will also put you in touch with both real estate professionals in your area, and with your classmates, people just like yourself who are beginning to invest in real estate. Take some classes. You'll be glad you did.

Along with taking classes, start building your own real estate library. While many of the books published on real estate promote formulas and easy roads to riches, they still include calculations that you may want for reference. If you approach them with some skepticism, you will be able to separate out the useful bits from the chaff. At the very least, you will begin to arm yourself against the snake-oil salesmen. Some of my favorite books on real estate are listed in the Appendix.

Here are some phrases for the first-time traveler in Real Estate Land. They should help you get through this chapter and ask good questions at open houses. I've included some tongue-in-cheek definitions—keep in mind that they may not be that far from reality.

Curb appeal *New paint and new landscaping. Be sure it's not new paint over old dry rot.*

Cozy *You can have either a bed or a dresser in the bedroom, not both.*

Creative touches of wallpaper *The seller papered over the cracks in the ceiling.*

Deferred maintenance, fixer-upper, TLC (tender loving care) needed, fixer, possibilities *Sometimes called a burner-downer. This place is in bad shape and the seller doesn't intend to do anything about it. Leave it to the professionals unless you have advanced skills and experience.*

Learning on the Internet You may live in an area where most of the information you want is already collected on web sites of the various real estate offices and the area's Multiple Listing Service. In that case you have your information neatly packaged already. Be sure to follow the trends for a month or so to get the feel of the market. The web site of the National Association of Realtors includes information on many areas of the country. Check it out, too.

The Jargon of Real Estate

Points, cap rate, loan to value, return on investment—a glance at the real estate section in any newspaper reveals an industry infested with jargon. As in other industries, real estate jargon evolved from abbreviations, shortcut terminology, and acronyms. Some of the terminology was adopted from the professions and services that support the real estate industry: property appraisal, land surveying, financing, marketing, building codes, accounting, and tax law. The contribution by each is specific to that industry. For example, your lender will talk about NOI, LTV, and cap rates, while your tax person wants to discuss accrued depreciation, balloon payments, and adjusted basis.

At first none of this will make sense to you as a new investor. But take heart! You really don't have to commit these terms to memory. There is no quiz on Friday. You just have to know where to find the definitions

Water view *If you climb up on the toilet in the second-floor bath you can get a glimpse of water out the window—if the neighbor's tree hasn't grown over the view yet.*

Bonus room *The builder didn't finish the room but we wanted to add the square footage to the cost.*

Pride of ownership *May include a yard full of plastic gnomes and deer or a kitchen covered with geese in blue gingham bows.*

when you need to use them.

I'll define the more technical terminology as I introduce it, an easier way to learn than by studying vocabulary lists. You'll also find a glossary at the end of the book. For page numbers telling where the subject is covered, you can also look in the Index. By the time you are ready to talk to a lender or make an offer, you'll be sounding like a pro.

A second kind of real estate jargon, marketing jargon, shows up in real estate ads. Marketing real estate is not much different from marketing soft drinks or SUVs. Ad writers use euphemisms, as well as trade jargon. In your first few tours of Real Estate Land, you may need a translator. As in any foreign language, you may know what the words mean, but unless you grasp the local idioms, you won't be able to figure out what the natives are really saying.

Filtered view *You could see the lake from here if you cut down that tree.*

Oldie but goodie, or vintage *Pink tile with black trim in the bath. A kitchen full of gold, avocado, or copper-tone appliances. Watch for lack of heating system and a foundation full of cracks.*

Easy-care yard *Covered with bark dust and three overgrown conifers, or possibly covered with ivy.*

RV parking *the entire yard is paved.*

Garage conversion *plan to park on the street. Also Den conversion.*

Keep in mind that real estate ads are designed to sell someone a place to rent, or a place to buy. If you know how to interpret sales and rental ads, you can add to your knowledge of the market. As I said earlier, these phrases tell an alert reader a great deal about the local rental market: *first month free, summer rates, no pets, no section 8, no smoking.* A light-hearted look at some of the advertising jargon used in selling real estate is in side bars throughout this chapter.

Educating yourself about both the sales market and the rental market requires life-long learning, if you are to be successful as a rental owner. Sometimes it will seem as if these two markets bear no financial relationship to each other. At the very least, one lags behind the other by as much as a couple of years. Only by tracking the trends will you begin to make sense of their relationship in your area.

You should study the sales market intensely for two or three months before you buy or sell, then review it every couple of months. Even after a transaction, you need to stay current with the rental market, and the ups, downs, and occasional side-wise movement of the market that will drive most of your day-to-day decisions. Keeping up with market trends will help you avoid costly mistakes, which will, in turn, make you a more confident, happier investor.

Learning the jargon will be easier; you will absorb it just from executing your investment plan, reading, and associating with other real estate professionals.

Summary

✔ You must learn about rents and vacancies in your local market.
✔ The jargon of real estate investing will seep into your brain as you study the markets. Soon you'll be speaking real estate like a native.
✔ The knowledge you gain from studying your local sales market will prevent serious mistakes and help you develop your investment plan.

■ *On the Internet*

www.nationalassociationofRealtors.com
www.Realtor.com
www.apartmentguide.com
www.homestore.com

Chapter 7

Find the **Right Property**

Chance favors the prepared mind.
LOUIS PASTEUR

A few years ago I fell in love with a sweet little duplex. Its arched doorways, coved ceilings, multi-paned windows, and hardwood floors were charming. It was a fixer-upper: just what I was looking for.

The roof of the duplex was shot, but I could handle that. The house had six inches of water standing under the floor, but I could handle that. My contractor's foot went through the bathroom floor, but I could handle that. Then my Realtor called and said, "Mabel, I've just noticed a 50,000-volt power line running right over the property. It goes to a big switching box behind the shrubs in the corner of the yard. Are you sure you want to make an offer?"

I couldn't handle that. People in my community are sensitive about high-voltage power lines. I would have trouble renting the property, and selling it would be a nightmare. Reason immediately overcame my emotional response, and I began to look for a more appropriate property. The rental I want to buy is the right property, in the right place, for the right price, at the right time. I'm sure that's what you want, too.

Before you start your hunt, review your financial goals and remind yourself of your specific criteria—those that define the right property for you. Will your income support a negative cash flow? Putting money into a property every month is called *feeding the alligator* in real estate jargon.

Do you need to find a modest property and live in one unit in order to get started? Can you pay cash for your purchase? Or, is your financial situation somewhere in between? The neighborhood and the price range in which you search for a rental to buy will depend on your financial situation and goals.

Here are the decisions you need to make before you start your search:

- Decide on your timing. Are you ready to buy now?
- Pick two or three neighborhoods in which to concentrate your search.
- Decide on the size and configuration of property that will meet your criteria.
- Choose a price range consistent with your financial plan.
- Decide on your financing terms: the amount down and the terms of the loan.

How to Find Rentals to Buy

Everyone who invests in real estate dreams of the piece of property they most want available for a song. That dream can come true, but only if you are prepared. Unless you have a clear picture of your dream property, you may not recognize it when it appears. That clear picture includes price, location, configuration, financing, and timing—and maybe coved ceilings and hardwood floors as well.

You can increase your odds of finding good properties by increasing the number of people who know what you want to buy. People buying and selling rental properties make up a small percentage of the population. Many of those people know each other and frequently exchange properties among themselves. The kind of properties you'd like to own may change hands without ever being publicly on the market.

Networks Work   My maintenance man Jim just bought his dream four-plex. The maintenance coordinator at a local property management firm knew what kind of property Jim was looking for. When one of the firm's clients said he was ready to sell, Jim was one of the first to find out. That's networking

One way to be a part of a network, and one of the first to hear about a good property, is to join your local rental-owner organization. These are the people who own, buy, and sell rental properties, usually the smaller ones. If you are a member and attend meetings, you may be in the room when someone announces that he or she is ready to sell the very property you want. In larger cities, owners' organizations often publish newsletters where members advertise their properties for sale. You need to be part of this network.

Tell your friends what you are looking for and where. They may know someone who knows someone. They may drive by a newly listed property and report to you that they saw a for sale sign.

Read, Read, Read   Check out bulletin boards, especially in your desired areas. If you live in a college town, check the bulletin boards on campus and at the local Laundromat.

Read both the for rent and the for sale the ads in your newspapers. Subscribe to your city's business newspaper, and read the alternative papers in your area. Read all the brochures and catalogs put out by your local Realtors. You'll find stands full of these publications near coffee shops and cafes, in real estate offices, and in motels and other tourist centers. Most of the ads in these little catalogs are for single-family homes, but you will often find small rental units included.

And what, you may ask, is your real estate agent doing while you are looking for a property to buy? Your agent is also searching for the perfect rental for you, but in different places. As I've mentioned, many properties are never advertised, my new six-plex for example. Your agent will be scouting out these un-advertised listings in her own office and others so she can alert you to properties available—before the ads make it into the newspapers or catalogs. She'll be announcing that she has a buyer for a certain type of property to her office colleagues, the Multiple Listing Service, and at breakfast and lunch meetings with other agents.

Properties that are *for sale by owner* won't be listed in a real estate office. Your agent finds these properties the same way you do—by reading the ads or driving by for sale signs. Unfortunately, I know several real estate agents who never read newspaper ads. Unless you have retained a buyer's agent, and perhaps even then, you need to do much of this research yourself. Drive through your target neighborhoods and look for signs and read the publications consistently.

> *Imagination is more important than knowledge.*
> ALBERT EINSTEIN

Many real estate offices, especially in larger cities, have web pages, as do most larger multiple listing agencies. Internet addresses for your local real estate offices and multiple listing agencies are printed on the brochures you picked up. If you can't find them, call the printed phone numbers and ask. One advantage of researching listings on the Internet is that you can sort listings by size, price, and location—a real labor-saving feature for you.

Public Records Some real estate gurus suggest searching public records for properties where owners are in arrears, or close to default, on their property taxes. For me these searches take up far more time than they are worth. If you see a property you are interested in, however, you can search the public records for the name and address of the owners. Write to the owners and inquire about the possibility of their selling the property—the worst they can do is ignore you.

Tax assessments are public records. To find names and address-es of owners, go to your local property-tax office, an escrow office, or your public library. In most cities escrow services will print out a document showing the owner of the property, the most recent tax assessment, and survey information that gives the precise location of the parcel. These documents are usually free of charge and known as *list kits*, or *triplets*.

Market Price vs Investment Value

To find your first property to purchase, eliminate all those that don't fit your criteria. Then evaluate those that do meet your needs to find the best choice. When you are ready to analyze properties on your *short list* as possible purchases, you will need some standards for comparison.

As you identify and analyze properties, you may find that your idea of value does not match the seller's. I like to think that the *price* of a property is what the seller wants, and the *value* is what I'm will-ing to pay for it. These numbers may be the same. They may be fair-ly close to each other. Or, they may be miles apart. Only you can set the investment value a property has for you, based on your goals and circumstances.

Investment-Value Formulas In order to compare properties and eliminate those outside your parameters, you need real numbers. Two of the simplest comparisons are *price per unit* and *gross income multiplier* (GIM). Price per unit is just as simple as it sounds. Divide the price by the number of units and you get price per unit.

The second number, GIM, is more refined and lets you include more information when comparing properties of widely differing prices and configurations. GIM is defined, roughly, as the number of years required for the gross rental income to pay off the purchase price of the property. It assumes the property is owned free and clear and does not include operating costs or debt service.

For example, suppose you see three properties you like, but they are so different you can't compare them easily. There is a nice duplex for $189,000, a four-plex for $191,500 and a six-plex for $224,000. The duplex and four-plex have similar prices, but the number of units and rents are very different. How does the larger unit, the six-plex, compare when everything about it is different from the other two? It is time to use the GIM.

■ Gross Income Multiplier Table

Units	Price	$/Unit	Rent/Unit	Annual Rent	GIM
2	$189,000	$94,500	$715	$17,400	11.0
4	191,500	47,875	525	25,260	7.6
6	224,000	37,333	445	32,040	7.0

From the table, you can see that the six-plex appears to be the best investment, since the gross rents would pay off the price in 7 years, while the duplex would take 11 years, and the four-plex, 7.6 years. Now you need to ask, "Which of these properties will provide sufficient cash flow to pay off the mortgage I will put on the property?" That calculation includes all the costs of ownership: maintenance, vacancy losses, debt service, property taxes, insurance, and other expenses.

Even a property listed for a *reasonable* price may not work for you if the expenses or the financing costs are too high. Much of your decision will be based on your debt service, which in turn, depends on the amount of money you borrow to buy your property. If possible, you would like to have enough cash flow to pay the mortgage payment and still put money in your pocket. For the six-plex above, the numbers might look like this:

■ *Rental Investment Analysis Sheet*

Property description: six-plex, rent = $500/mo/unit

Annual rental income

Annual scheduled rent	$36,000
Minus vacancy/credit loss	1,800
Total annual income	**34,200**

Annual expenses

Maintenance, taxes, and utilities	13,680
(When estimating, use 40% of net rents)	
Net operating income (cash flow)	**20,520**
Minus debt service	12,048
($120,000 loan @ 8% and 20 years)	
Your cash flow	**$8,472**

A lower debt service means more cash flow to you, but a lower rate of return on your investment—you invested more to buy the property. A higher debt service means smaller cash flow to you, higher return on your investment, and higher risk. Your decision about a property depends on the relationship between rents, cost of upkeep, and debt service.

Net operating income (NOI) is a number investors use, along with *cap rate*, to estimate value of a property. NOI and cap rate are more frequently applied to larger complexes, those of more than four or six units.

Making accurate comparisons is difficult if the seller is less than forthcoming about real rents and expenses. You may see ads insisting "rents could be higher" for a property. This is where your careful study of your market will pay off. Could the rents be higher? Can you rely on the seller telling you what the rents really are?

You will make your offer to purchase contingent on the seller disclosing the real rents. It would save time, however, if you could have that information before you make your offer. When the information is not forthcoming, you have to depend on your own research. If you have studied the rents in the area, you'll have a good idea of the rent you could get for a property, and you can use those numbers in your value calculations.

When I bought my most recent purchase, a turn-of-the-century six-plex, the seller had gone to a Realtor for a *comparative market analysis*, a price-range valuation for the property. In order to estimate a selling price, the Realtor assumed that some of the space could be rented as office space and suggested a price range for the complex between $283,000 and $340,000. I did not believe that office space could be rented for the amount the Realtor set and was prepared to give up on the purchase.

Fortunately, the seller decided to get an appraisal as a way to set the price. The appraiser also knew there was a great deal of empty office space near this property, and he based his appraised value on converting the empty space to a residential unit instead. The appraised value was $245,000, quite different from the Realtor's estimate. The more reasonable price allowed me to borrow enough additional money to refurbish the units. The improved appearance and livability increased the rents, increased cash flow, and gave me a property I am proud to own.

Tax Assessments A piece of information you may find useful when you're trying to set a value on a piece of property is the value set by your property-taxing authority. Acquaint yourself with your local tax office and learn to find the information on specific pieces of property. Use tax assessment information cautiously. Budget reductions have reduced staff levels at most tax offices, so on-site inspections have slowed. Some properties may not be physically inspected for seven or eight years.

Reduced staff also means more shortcuts are used between

inspections to calculate the value used to set the property taxes. Assessors use general formulas for estimating rent increases, maintenance costs, and other variables, as a way to set value for a property. If the property owner did major cosmetic work, installing new carpets and vinyl, and painting the interior just after the last on-site inspection, he probably raised the rents accordingly. The property value assigned would not account for the improvements, and the tax would suggest a lower than realistic value.

Conversely, if some major problem developed after the last inspection, the tax would not reflect the decreased value caused by the problem. The value used to set property taxes is one more piece of information for your analysis. It may help you, but you should not rely on it solely.

The Eyeball Test

So now you have your list pared down to three to five possible purchases, based on the numbers. It is time to apply the eyeball test, a potentially sticky point when buying rentals. It is not unusual for a property owner to refuse to allow you to inspect the interior of rental units until after you have submitted an offer to purchase.

You can see the property owner's logic. Why disturb the tenants for sightseers who are not serious buyers? But how do you, the serious buyer, cope? You learn as much as you can without disturbing the tenants, and you make sure that one of your conditions, if and when you do make an offer, is the *"buyer's approval of conditions found on a full and complete inspection of all interior and exterior spaces, by all persons deemed necessary in the buyer's sole discretion."*

You can do and should do a great deal of exterior inspection yourself as part of your process of eliminating undesirable properties. Drive by the property at different times during the day *and* night. Remember that good neighbors will help you keep good tenants.

Make notes on these items:

The Property
- Building and yard maintenance.
- Level of clutter. Tenants who are messy and careless on the outside may be messy and careless with the inside. Mess may not be an issue, but careless renters cause damage.
- The number of cars parked around. Describe them and the places they are parked so you can tell if they have been moved during the day. Watch for cars up on blocks.

The Neighborhood
- Noise level, especially later in the evening.
- Proximity of conveniences such as public transportation, shopping, libraries, and other services.
- Presence of sidewalks, play areas, and parks.
- Number of similar rental units in the same area.

In my community, and perhaps in yours, developments with clusters of duplexes or four- plexes seem to become seedy-looking rather rapidly. Small complexes interspersed with single-family homes may hold their value longer. The number of isolated duplexes and four-plexes you find depends on your local zoning. My community zoning allows construction of a duplex on any corner lot that is large enough. That means nice duplexes can be found in some attractive neighborhoods. Drop into your building department and find out how duplexes and four-plexes are treated in your community.

Make notes when you drive. Take pictures. But don't trespass, and don't talk to tenants at this point. Owners rightly fear having tenants know that they are thinking of selling. Since tenants often believe their rents will go up as soon as a property sells, many will give a 30-day move-out notice if they discover that their unit will be sold.

Because your offer to purchase will address the condition of the building(s) and include remedies and negotiating points, I'll cover those items in Chapter 8 when I talk about making your offer. I'll give you list of ways to spot misleading information from both sellers and Realtors about conditions, rents, and costs. I'll also make some suggestions about how to deal with a property you want but think is overpriced.

As an investor, you want to find the right property, at the right price, in the right place, at the right time. You'll increase your chances of finding that property if you let everyone know what you want, and do you homework with the newspaper, the computer, and the car.

Summary

✔ Set your search parameters—neighborhoods, price, and configuration—before you start your search.

✔ Network with friends and other rental owners. Let everyone know what you want to buy and where.

✔ Read your local newspaper and real estate publications to find properties that fit your purchase criteria.

✔ Drive your target neighborhoods weekly.

✔ Use listed prices of rentals and estimated expenses to calculate GIM and NOI as a way to compare properties.

✔ Check out the property-tax information on properties that interest you.

■ *On the Internet*

For help with identifying your target neighborhoods try:

www.HomeAdvisor.com   **www.Realtor.com**
www.homeseekers.com   **www.homeadvisor.com**

A nationwide listing is *Homes & Land*, a magazine offering listings across the country. Find them at **www.HomesAndLand.com** or call 800-277-7800.

Part Three

The Trans-
Action

Chapter 8 | # *Make the* Offer to Purchase

Caveat emptor. (Let the buyer beware.)
UNKNOWN

I hope you read this chapter long before you find your first rental to purchase. Knowing what is entailed in the offer may help you eliminate some properties from consideration. It is disheartening to get ready to make an offer and then find there are things about the property, the financing, or the seller's requirements that make the property less than ideal for you. You'll save your time and the Realtor's if you're somewhat familiar with the process.

The Paperwork

You may find that making your first offer to buy a rental is intimidating—all those forms, many of them new and unfamiliar. Once you know what each form does, however, and how the process should go, you will find the paperwork more straightforward.

Each form is designed to meet the needs of one of the three parties to the transaction: you, the buyer; the seller, represented by a Realtor; and the lender, the financial institution lending you the money.

The Offer to Purchase The first form you will see as a buyer of rental property is the *offer to purchase* or the *earnest money form*. You use this form to communicate to the seller the price you are offering to pay for the property, the down payment you're prepared to pay, any time constraints you have, the amount and form of earnest money you are offering, and any contingencies associated with your offer. The offer to purchase can be several pages long.

Your offer to purchase is your opening move in your negotiation with the seller. In response to your offer, the seller may accept all your conditions, may reject all your conditions, or may send back a *counter offer* in which he or she asks for negotiation on any or all points.

The offer to purchase or earnest money form spells out the details of the transaction. In most states, the agency that oversees real estate transactions requires standardized language for most of the details. You can find a sample offer to purchase form on my website **www.investinrentalproperty.com.** Working through the items on the form may seem pretty tedious, but keep in mind that each item is there to protect somebody. I'll relate a few war stories as we go along to illustrate the need for that protection.

1. The purchase price and conditions At the top of the form you will indicate how much you are offering for the property, how you plan to pay for it, the amount of down payment you are offering, and preliminary details about any financing you expect to obtain.

You should have already discussed these issues with your lender and with your Realtor. If the sales market is hot, another buyer could come in and buy the property while you work to come up with your financing.

Depending on the terms of the financing you expect to obtain, your lender may require a minimum amount of down payment, although you can always offer more than the minimum. The investment plan you developed in Chapter 4 should include a projected down payment amount based on your plan.

2. The earnest money A seller wants to sell the property, get the money, and move on. To ensure a seller that you are serious about buying the property, you put up earnest money, essentially a bond guaranteeing your good intentions. Your earnest money, also called a *good-faith offer*, says that you are earnest in your offer, and that you agree to forfeit that money if you back out of the deal for some trivial reason. You'll see further on in the form, that the earnest money amount will be subtracted from your down payment.

Obviously the seller, and probably the listing Realtor, want you to put up as much earnest money as possible. They want a guarantee that you won't back out of the deal for a frivolous reason. You, of course, want to tie up as little money as you can while the transaction is taking place—I've known transactions

> *Pay peanuts and you get monkeys.*
> ANONYMOUS

to take as long as four months to close. I'd like to have my money making interest for me during that time rather than sitting in the Realtor's client-trust account, as I'm sure you would.

Two ways to help you keep your money from being tied up for long periods are to offer as little as possible, and/or to make the earnest money offer as a promissory note rather than a check. You should discuss your plans with your Realtor before you get to the transaction stage.

I bought my first couple of duplexes with $250 in earnest money. They had already been repossessed by a bank that was desperate to get rid of them. The bank would take almost anything a buyer would offer as earnest money, even $250.

Five years later, when the market was on the rebound, a Realtor assured me her office required a minimum of $1000 for earnest money. When I expressed my sympathy about their losing a deal over such a rule, the amount quickly dropped to the $400 I had been prepared to deposit. If your Realtor works from an office with a minimum earnest money amount, you should find out what that amount is, then decide if you can live with it.

However much you deposit as earnest money, you don't want to lose it. A number of escape clauses that will help you protect your earnest money deposit appear farther down on the printed form. These may not be enough to make you feel completely secure, however. An addendum form will let you list your own terms and conditions for your purchase. I'll suggest some language to use on addenda to help protect your deposit if the deal falls through.

3. Legal descriptions Your offer to purchase is a legal contract. As such it must state in specific detail what is being bought and sold, hence the legal description. It isn't enough to just say you want to buy the duplex at 450 Malibar. The site must be described in standard surveyor language, using metes and bounds to give the specific location of the site on the planet. Additional descriptions on the form apply to the building itself, any additional buildings on the site, and any personal property that might be included.

Read the legal description carefully. Be sure to inspect the property to see if any structures appear to encroach on neighboring property. Make sure there are no encroachments from other properties, or private or public easements. At the very least, encroachments and easements can hold up the title insurance and your financing. At worst, these issues can produce endless court battles, both at the time of purchase and at any time you might want to remodel, expand, or sell.

I once spent weeks trying to convince a lender that the telephone pole at the corner of a 14-story building was not an encroachment that would cause problems with the ninth-floor condo I wanted to buy. At the same time I had to convince them that a ninth-floor condo really didn't need flood insurance, so perhaps that lender tended to overreact.

In the best of all worlds your Realtor should have already looked into all these legal issues. Buyers who rely on the Realtor to have done all the work, however, may end up in legal trouble.

Doing your homework is called doing *due diligence* in the legal world. If you try to sue the seller or the Realtor later for some undisclosed problem, they may be able to show that you didn't do your own due diligence, and keep you from collecting damages. Remember you are your own best friend.

4. Conveyance form and use restrictions The earnest money form will have space for you to specify the kind of *title conveyance* you intend to use. The *title conveyance form* describes the property, any use restrictions attached to the property, the terms of purchase, and the buyer's name. It is the form that will be recorded in the public records showing you as the new owner of the property. The forms of title conveyance depend on the state where the transaction takes place. Some states use a *trust deed.* Others use a *mortgage,* but the general characteristics will be the same. Your Realtor will let you know which form is required in your state.

Read a couple of standard conveyance forms carefully before you make an offer. You want to know how they work. And, you need to know how the title of the property you want to buy was transferred to the current owner. You should have a copy of the seller's current deed to read before you get to closing. Be sure you are familiar with any use restrictions and financial obligations carried by the deed. These documents give new meaning to the word tedious, but you need to know what is in them. Once you have waded through one set, you can usually just skim them in the future because they are all similar.

> *Only a fool thinks price and value are the same.*
> ANTONIO MACHADO

If the property is a part of a *planned unit development* (PUD), numerous restrictions may apply, all of which will be itemized in a form called the *covenants, codes, and restrictions* (CC&Rs). A copy of the CC&Rs should be available for you to study *before* you make an offer. They may include provisions that prohibit you from renting your property to anyone else. They may prevent you from selling to anyone under 55 years of age. They may prohibit you, or your renter, from changing the color of the drapes or hanging laundry outside to dry.

Condos and many new developments are PUDs. Be sure you can live with the restrictions if you buy into a PUD.

> *Sometimes your best invest-*
> *ments are the ones you*
> *don't make.*
> DONALD TRUMP

Other weird restrictions may be included on deeds. Perhaps Grandpa was a teetotaler and thought the rest of the world should be too. He may have stipulated in the deed that no alcohol could be consumed on the property. Yes, Grandpa may have done that. If you serve champagne at your daughter's wedding reception, Grandpa's heirs could sue and cause you to lose the property. Be sure you know what is in the deed to the property you are buying.

5. What you are buying The property you are offering to buy is divided into components. First is the *land*, the lot the building(s) sits on, described legally by metes and bounds. The buildings on the land, along with everything attached permanently to them, are called *improvements*, and classified as *real property*. Anything not attached to the buildings or the land is called *personal property*. Every component can be, and has been, argued about.

What constitutes the real property you are about to purchase should be clear cut, but it may not be. Most states include light fixtures and window-covering hardware as real property. They are attached to the walls, ceilings, and window frames, after all. If you have any concern that the seller doesn't define real property the same way you do, make sure you spell out in your offer to purchase what you expect to remain in the building. The law would probably be on your side if the seller removes real property, but you would prefer not to have to go to court to get the curtain rods back.

My Realtor tells about a client who bought a beautifully land-scaped home. After closing the buyer found out that the sellers had set big flowering shrubs—in pots—into the yard to give the land-scape a boost. After the buyer signed the deal, the seller moved out the potted plants and left the new owner with a landscape full of bomb craters. This is an extreme example, and you shouldn't have to go around the yard tugging on the shrubs. But it does give you a sense of the extent some sellers will go to.

6. *Personal property* includes everything not attached to a building. When purchasing rental property, be sure to ask about owner-ship of the kitchen appliances. You may not be able to imagine why the seller wants six stoves and six refrigerators, but don't leave it to chance. Make sure your offer to purchase includes descriptions of the appliances you expect to find when you take possession. I got a real shock when I had to evict a tenant and found the refrigerator in his unit belonged to him. Suddenly I had the cost of a new fridge along with the cost of the eviction.

If you are buying a property that is already a rental, a line on the form will allow the seller to indicate that tenant property is *not* included in the purchase, and to describe the tenant property. Be sure to ask about ownership of appliances.

7. *Closing in escrow* These lines indicate that a disinterested third party will draw up all the documents, make sure all the parties sign them, see to it that all the money gets to the right place, and properly record the documents that transfer title. A disinterested party is not someone bored with the proceedings. It is a person who has no financial interest in the transaction. Some of the documents you will sign we have already covered; others will be described in Chapter 9. Buyer and seller usually split the fee for this service, called *escrow service.*

The earnest money form will ask for the name of the escrow company where closing will take place. Your Realtor will probably have a favorite *closer*, and unless you have a reason to prefer a different firm, there is no reason not to follow that lead. If you think you are heading for a long, aggressive career in real estate investing, you might want to cultivate a relationship with a closer who specializes in tax-deferred exchanges.

8. The boiler plate About two-thirds of an offer to purchase is standard contract language, called boiler plate, that defines the conditions of the agreement. Every state and every real estate firm use slightly different wording, but most of it means much the same in the end. Be sure to read it carefully.

Toward the end of the boiler plate is a listing of the real estate brokers involved, their agreement regarding their fees, and the disposal of the earnest money if you end up forfeiting it. Under this is the line for the signature and mailing address of the buyer.

Your Conditions of Purchase: The Addenda

Earnest money forms seldom have enough space for a prospective buyer to list all her conditions of purchase. You will probably need to attach one or more addendum pages to your offer to buy. Say on the addendum that "purchase is contingent on the buyer's approval of these items."

Inspections Few of us have the knowledge and experience to ferret out all possible problems with the buildings we are buying. We rely on termite and dry rot (T&D) inspections, or whole-house inspections, where a licensed contractor inspects heating, mechanical, and electrical systems, as well as structural integrity.

The offer to purchase has a line indicating who will pay for such inspections, as well as a space to show who will pay for needed repairs. *You should plan to pay for inspections.* Even better, you should find an inspector who will allow you to follow him around as he does the inspection. Ask the inspector what he looks for, and where, and why. Notice the way he tests for dry rot, where he looks for water leakage, and how he spots evidence of insect infestation in the building. This is part of your education as an investor.

T&D inspections have been known to favor the party paying for the inspection, a good example of "who pays the piper calls the tune." If you pay, the inspector will see the termites that may have been invisible if the seller was paying. If you still have concerns after an inspection, get another one, from a different inspector.

The first multiplex I bought was examined by three different inspectors. The first, paid by the seller, found absolutely nothing wrong. The second, sought by a Realtor, discovered the need for extensive and costly insect extermination. I learned later that the second inspector ran an extermination business on the side. The third, an inspector I hired and supervised, found a small carpenter-ant infestation, dry rot in a couple of bathrooms,

> *Sometimes you win and sometimes you learn.*
> KIYOSAKI

and a couple of small roof leaks. I've owned the building more than ten years and have had no indication of other insect or dry rot problems. I'm glad I paid for the third inspection.

Because passing off dry-rot and termite problems to unsuspecting buyers is such a grand old tradition, many states now require *seller disclosure forms.* In Oregon the form is four pages long. The seller indicates what he or she knows about each item, from the condition of the roof to the stability of the foundation Of course, there is a column titled "unknown" which gives the seller some wiggle room. It does, however, give the buyer some leverage when a problem is found and needs to be corrected. If your state doesn't require disclosure forms, make up your own and be sure you've addressed all the issues.

Better yet, hire a *whole-house inspector* to give you a professional estimate of the condition of the property. Whole-house inspectors who are certified by a national firm do not do repair work on the side and have less conflict of interest. The inspector normally wants to go over the inspection report with the prospective buyer to discuss the findings and sometimes possible solutions. References at the end of this chapter list whole-house inspectors.

As soon as the seller accepts your offer, you need to make a "full and complete" inspection of all areas of the property. Your initial inspection may have been enough to prompt you to make an offer; now you need more specific and detailed information about the property. Carry a notepad and pen and plan to spend a couple of hours in your inspection. Make notes about anything you want a licensed inspector to give special attention: sponginess around toilets and sinks, discoloration on ceilings, discoloration on bath and kitchen floors. Note the age of the appliances and check the installation date of the water heater. If these appliances seem old enough to need replacement soon, your cash flow calculations may need to be adjusted. Or you may want to negotiate with the seller for some discount for older appliances.

> *A verbal contract isn't worth the paper it's written on.*
> Samuel Goldwyn

Following your own inspection, have a licensed inspector conduct a whole-house inspection. Make your purchase conditional on your approval of that inspection report. You can't know ahead of time what an inspection will reveal. Also consider asking for a home warranty. That way, if the dishwasher quits a week after you take possession, you'll be able to get some help with the cost of repairing or replacing it.

Income and Expense Verification   You need to approve or verify all rents and expenses. Ask for a *rent roll*, a list of all existing tenants, their terms of rent or lease, and the rents they pay. You may want to ask to see the seller's Schedule C from his most recent tax return.

Your decision to make the offer to buy was based on the rents you expect to get and on the seller's declared expenses. Be sure to verify the numbers.

Listing your conditions of purchase gives you a way to terminate a transaction without giving specific details. By requiring that you approve of rents or an inspection report, the way is left open for you to simply not approve, thereby ending the transaction. If you feel there is something wrong, but can't put your finger on it, don't hesitate to back out. Most people have pretty good intuition. Pay attention to yours.

The Process

As soon as you let your Realtor know that you want to make an offer on a property, she should order a list kit. When you meet with the Realtor to write up the offer, look over the list kit to make sure there are no surprises lurking in the property description, the deed, or the previous terms of financing.

Writing up an offer will take a couple of hours as you discuss the details of the property, your offer, your financing, and your conditions of purchase. Once you sign the offer, the Realtor makes an appointment with the seller to "present" your offer. You will have typically given the seller five to ten days to respond to your offer, unless the market is busy, in which case, you may give the seller just 24 hours.

As you wait for the seller to respond, your Realtor may contact you with questions from the seller, or you may not hear anything. Don't hesitate to call your Realtor, but try not to be a pest. These things take time. While you wait, however, you should be completing your financing package. If the seller accepts your offer, along with your conditions, immediately order the professional inspections and schedule your own detailed inspection of the property.

Depending on the conditions discovered on inspection, you

may reject the property, accept everything, or enter into negotiations with the seller about what repairs need to be done and who pays for them.

Negotiating Your Purchase   Suppose you discovered dry rot in the floor of one bathroom in the duplex you want to buy. Most lenders insist that repairs be done before they lend money to buy a property. You and the seller can handle the repairs any way you choose, from "seller pays for all of it," to "buyer pays for all of it." You need to agree—in writing—about who pays for what, and when. Because the total cost of such repairs is difficult to estimate, you may want to include language that stipulates your top limit. For example: *buyer pays for dry-rot repair in master bathroom to a total of no more than $750. Seller pays for all dry-rot repair in master bathroom beyond $750.*

In most communities reputable contractors adhere to accepted standards for structural repairs. If your Realtor suggests several names of contractors to do repairs, you can be fairly confident that the work will meet code. Dry-rot contractors usually expect to be paid at closing, so you don't have to put the money up front even if you agree to pay for the repair.

Cosmetic issues are another matter. You may hate the orange shag carpet in the family room, but you probably shouldn't insist the seller replace it. Buyers are almost always unhappy about carpet or paint selected by the seller, and you don't want the person who chose orange shag in the first place to choose new carpet for you. Ask instead for a "carpet allowance" reduction in the price.

The seller of a rental property has many reasons for selling. You have reasons for buying and for the terms and conditions listed in your offer. If you and the seller, through her agent, can discuss your reasons, you may be able to work out a transaction that addresses both sets of needs. Try to find out what the seller needs from the transaction and think about how you can accommodate those needs.

Once you and the seller have agreed on the conditions of the sale, send a written statement saying that your conditions have been met and you are waiving the contingencies. Some real estate offices use forms, otherwise, your Realtor will help you draft the letter.

Closing the Transaction Once you have waived your conditions, your Realtor sends the documents to the escrow office, while you finish the last of your financing paper work. When your lender sends a loan commitment letter to you, with a copy to escrow, the closer will call you to set an appointment to sign all the closing documents. The escrow closer will tell you how much cash you will need to present in the form of a certified or cashier's check in order to close the transaction. You will also be required to present a binder from your insurance agent, a written commitment from the insurance company to provide hazard insurance for the property you are buying. The cost of the first year's insurance will be included in the closing costs.

Most Realtors expect to attend closing with their clients, especially first-time buyers of investment property. They will be there to answer questions, explain some of the complicated jargon, and generally hold the buyer's hand. I still have one of my Realtors at closing with me. I think two pairs of eyes are better than one when looking at financial and legal documents.

Summary

✔ The reams of paperwork involved in real estate transactions are designed to protect the parties to the transaction: you, the seller, and the lender.

✔ The earnest money form communicates to the seller what you are offering for a property and your terms and conditions for purchase.

✔ Terms not covered by the earnest money form, are listed on separate sheets called addenda.

✔ When negotiating the purchase of a rental property, consider the seller's needs as well as your own.

■ *On the Internet*

Home Inspection Resources:

American Institute of Inspectors (1-800-877-4770)
www.inspection.org

American Society of Home Inspectors (1-800-743-2744)
www.ashi.com

National Association of Home Inspectors (1-800-448-3942)
www.nahi.org

Inspect-A-Home Inspections
www.inspect-a-homeinspections.com

Chapter 9 | *Finance Your Purchase:* The Cash

If you can find a path with no obstacles, it probably doesn't lead anywhere.
FRANK A. CLARK

Chapter 3 pointed out the advantages of using other people's money to pay for part of your ticket to financial independence. Unless you have found a way to get someone else to pay for all of it, however, you will still need some cash. The amount of cash depends on the size of your loan, the down payment you make, and the loan costs. The total cash needed at closing, usually paid with a certified or cashier's check, is called the *closing costs*.

The Closing Costs: How Much Will You Need?

The money you need to close a transaction and transfer ownership to you consists of three chunks. One chunk, the down payment, goes directly to the seller. The lender and the escrow company take the second chunk for loan fees, the appraisal fee, the cost of preparing and recording documents, and the title insurance policy.

The last chunk of the closing costs is money associated with the property itself: the property taxes, hazard insurance, and the cost of repairs to the property, according to the split you and the seller have agreed upon.

Down Payment   The down payment is the largest amount of cash you need for your purchase. Fortunately, there are ways to reduce a down payment. I'll suggest some ideas later in this chapter, then enlarge on them in Chapter 10 when I talk about financing, since these ideas may involve the loan conditions.

Remember the example of Caitlin and her duplexes? Caitlin was able to borrow 90 percent of the purchase price because she bought each duplex on a residential loan. If the property you are buying does not qualify for a residential loan, you may have to get a commercial loan, pay more than 10 percent down, and borrow less than 90 percent. Down payments can range from 3 percent for FHA-guaranteed residential loans to 25 percent for some commercial properties. I'll describe the specifics for these loans more fully in Chapter 10.

Loan Costs   Lenders are required, by law, to provide you with a good-faith estimate of the cost of borrowing money from them. You'll find the estimate includes lots of little fees, many of which are a percentage of the loan.

If your purchase price is $100,000, your closing costs will be somewhere between $5,000 and $18,000, depending on the financing you obtain. For each additional $1,000 of purchase price, you can add a corresponding amount to the range of closing costs. The $5,000 is a low estimate and assumes you will be able to obtain good FHA financing and are planning to live in one unit of your property.

The high estimate reflects the closing costs you might face for a $100,000 purchase if you need to get a commercial loan with its increased fees, or if you live in a state that requires that an attorney take care of your closing. The higher closing costs required for commercial loans are one reason I suggest properties of four or fewer units for beginning investors. Unfortunately there is no way to avoid the higher fees charged by attorneys who do real property closings. Consult your Realtor about the requirements where you live and work the fee into your budget.

Here is a list of the items and the amounts I paid to the lender when I closed my most recent transaction:

■ *Closing Costs For a $310,000 Loan*

Loan costs	Loan origination cost (loan fee)	$3,500
	Commercial appraisal	900
	Document preparation	50
Property cost	Property taxes (pro-rated)	1,575
	Hazard insurance	650
Escrow cost	Title insurance policy (one half)	250
	Escrow processing	150
	Deed recording	25
	Miscellaneous recording	25
Total closing costs		**$7,125**

Where to Look for Cash

You may be surprised at the number of places to find cash to begin investing in rental property. The sources of cash listed below are in order of my own preferences.

The Seller There are several options involving the seller.

1. You might be able to assume the owner's current loan, though few assumable mortgage loans have been made since the 1980s. If you find an assumable loan, it will be an older loan with a small balance, and you may still have to borrow some money to purchase the

property. Sellers and lenders are more eager to accommodate your desire to assume a loan when interest rates are higher. It is worth trying at any time, however, since it can save you loan fees, appraisal fees, and some of the other incidental fees. Your down payment must cover the seller's equity in some manner; see number 2.

2. Get the seller to carry all or part of the down payment as a second mortgage. You can ask for seller financing when you make your offer, either as a part of assuming the existing loan or as part of an offer which includes a new loan. Your lender will have some guidelines about how much they will allow you to borrow on a second mortgage, and some lenders prohibit second mortgages. Your lender may insist that the total loans against a property be no more than a certain percentage of the property value. Be sure to talk to your lender before you commit yourself.

3. You may be able to talk a motivated seller into paying some of the closing costs in order to make a sale. When a property has been on the market for some time, the seller is often willing to "sweeten" the deal to get a sale. Remember, if you don't ask, you won't get it.

4. The seller might be willing to carry the entire contract, in which case, the down payment is completely negotiable. This may or may not save you money. You may be able to negotiate terms that are favorable to you, but you will need to have an attorney draw up the contract to be sure that both you and the seller are fully protected. Depending on the complexities of the contract, the legal fees may be more than the amount you'd have spent going through an institutional lender.

Your Own Home If you own your home, your equity is one of your best sources of cash, both in the amount that may be available and the cost to you of using it. Unlike consumer loans, such as credit card lines of credit, the interest you pay on any real estate loan is tax-deductible. A loan against your equity in your own residence qualifies. You can use your home equity to provide cash in several ways.

■ *Go Figure*

How Much of Your Home's Equity Can You Borrow?

Here's how to calculate the amount you may be able to borrow against the equity in your residence:

1. The market value of your home   _____
   (find this number on your tax statement)

2. Multiply line 1 by .80, .85, or .90   _____
   (the percent of market value
   your lender will lend)

3. Subtract the current balance of your   _____
   mortgage from line 2. (include any other
   mortgages, liens, or encumbrances)

4. The remainder is the amount you may   _____
   be able to borrow against your equity

1. You might take out an equity loan and place a second mortgage on your home. You may be able to obtain an equity loan from the lender that holds the present mortgage, or you may go to a new lender. Either way, the holder of your first mortgage may have to agree to allow a second mortgage. Give your mortgage holder a call and ask if they will make a home-equity loan.

The maximum amount available to you for a second mortgage loan will be a percentage of the current value of your home, less the existing mortgage balance. You will be asked to pay for an appraisal in order to set the value. You may also have to declare what you intend to use the money for when you fill out the loan application form.

2. You may refinance your entire mortgage. At the current low interest rates, refinancing might allow you to obtain the cash you want for investment and still not increase your mortgage payments very much. All the same conditions apply to refinancing—the need for an independent valuation and a closing transaction with the attending costs.

3. You may obtain an *equity line of credit*. A line of credit is something like a loan, and something like a revolving charge account. You apply for a line of credit the same way you do for refinancing, but the loan doesn't go into effect until you want the money. Normally you will be issued a set of checks when your loan closes, then you write checks on the account just as if it were a checking account. Those checks constitute money you are borrowing against the value of your home. That loan must be repaid according to the agreement you signed when you got the line of credit.

You should shop for an equity line of credit in the same way you would shop for a loan, since you will face many of the same costs. Here is a list of the fees you need to compare:

- Percentage rate, either fixed or variable.
- Draw period.
- Repayment period.
- Closing costs.
- Renewal availability.

An equity line of credit is a good choice if you want to arrange for the cash now, but are not ready to buy. Lines of credit give you maximum flexibility in the amount of money you borrow. And except for a set minimum payment, the line of credit also allows you flexibility in the speed with which you pay off the balance.

Your Family and Your Friends   Next to your own home, your friends and family may be your best source of cash for buying rentals. Is there a family member who might make you a gift of the down payment? Could someone in the family lend you the money? Is there someone who would like to participate in the purchase as a joint venture? If you don't ask, you will never know.

Two things to remember about money matters and family: First, you must make all agreements in writing and be sure that all parties understand them and sign them. Have an attorney draw up the agreement; it will be worth the money. Not putting financial agreements in writing suggests a less than professional approach, and casual agreements have too often led to serious family problems.

Second, you must be sure you know how the IRS will treat your agreement. Ask your tax consultant about gift tax guidelines from the IRS. Ask too, about how the interest you pay a family member for a loan will be treated, and how the lender should declare the interest as income. If done right, a family loan is straight forward. If not done right, you could both be audited and face penalties.

Yourself If neither your home nor your family can provide cash, you may have to settle in for the long haul while you use your own resources to accumulate enough cash to start building your real estate empire. You may have already committed yourself to watching your spending more closely after developing your financial goals, but it won't hurt to review some specifics. Many people are amazed to realize just how much they spend for

> *If your ship doesn't come in, swim out to it.*
> JONATHAN WINTERS

things that don't mean much to them. Some life-style changes can lead to cash accumulation faster than you might have dreamed.

Start with your credit cards. The average American owes $7,000 on credit cards, and few people pay off their balance every 30 days. Most pay just the minimum. The result is that at the usual interest rate of somewhere around 18 percent, the average American is making a minimum payment of about $650 per month. Add a yearly fee and late fees to that, and the payment may be closer to

$675 a month.

Now, $675 may or may not seem like much money each month. When you multiply that monthly payment by 12 months, however, you begin to see the significance. In one year, the payments amount to $8,100. Look at that! By the end of two years, the average American has spent $16,200 on credit card payments *without bringing the balance down much, if at all.*

Only a fool tests the depth of the water with both feet.
AFRICAN PROVERB

Suppose you are one of those average Americans. If you did not charge another thing on that card and stretched a bit to pay it off in a year, you could then put $675 into an interest-bearing account every month. At the end of two years you would have enough cash to buy a small property.

I'm not going to tell you to cut up your credit cards and throw away the pieces. I agree with the Gardner brothers, authors of the *Motley Fool* financial guides. They suggest you pay off your credit cards, then divide your purchases into three categories: emergencies, necessities, and luxuries. If you use your credit card only for emergencies and pay off the balance every month, you save the 18 percent interest—which is the same as earning 18 percent.

Two more bad habits could be slowing your drive to financial independence, smoking and buying lottery tickets. Let's look first at lottery tickets, which may not cost you as much as cigarettes, but certainly won't put any money in your investments.

When my son was a junior high school student, he took a class in probability and statistics. The teacher described the way lotteries worked and asked the kids to figure out how to win. My son came home, announced that he was going to tell me how to beat the lottery, and disappeared into his room with his computer. When he emerged a couple of hours later, the first thing he said was, "Don't buy lottery tickets." The second was, of course, "What's for dinner?" I decided that if a 13-year-old could figure out there was no way to play the lottery and win, I wouldn't even consider it.

Smoking may seem more a health than a financial issue until you look at it in the same light as credit cards. Cigarettes cost about $45 a carton in Oregon. If you smoke one carton a week, however, you spend more than $2,000 every year. Even if you stuffed that $45 in your mattress every week instead of smoking it, you could buy an investment property in a couple of years.

Time to Be Really Creative Now, suppose you don't have any bad habits, not any expensive ones anyway. You don't have family members eager to give you money, and you always treat your credit cards like 30-day charges. Where are you going to find cash for a real estate venture? You obviously have a greater challenge and will need to be creative. Here are some ways other people have boot-strapped themselves into rental investments.

1. Offer some *sweat equity*. It is sometimes possible to trade your own labor for some portion of the down payment. You paint the interior or exterior of the property you want to buy, or you agree to do all the termite and dry rot repair in lieu of a down payment. Depending on the needs of the property and the seller, and your own skills and time, your efforts can multiply the impact of a small amount of cash. The lender may, however, insist on using only licensed contractors for actual structural repairs. Be sure to ask.

2. You may need to *tighten your belt* with regard to your own spending. Look at your spending patterns again and see where you might make some cuts that would allow you to build up a cash reserve to start your investment career. Some ideas:

- Muriel Siebert, the first woman to own a seat on the New York Stock Exchange, advises women to take an amount equal to what they spent on the most expensive clothing item they bought in any given month and put it into an investment account.

- Study your phone bills. Do you really need a cell phone? Can you use a calling card for long distance?
- Figure out how much you spend in a year if you have even one daily $2.75 latte.
- Can you find a way to have a family pizza night without dropping $50 at the pizza parlor every week?
- Make a list of your weekly or monthly expenses: manicures, haircuts, movies, lunches and dinners out, and subscriptions or newsstand purchases. Little things add up fast.
- A friend who works in downtown Seattle arranged with a co-worker to bring leftovers for lunches and share. She also carries coffee from home, rather than stopping at espresso stands. Altogether, she estimates that she now saves close to $70 a week on those two items alone.

3. Finally, you may need to look into a part-time, temporary job. A friend of mine took a paper route for a year. It was a good choice, letting her be home when the kids were, but giving her three to four hours of work a day. At the end of the year she had enough to make her first purchase.

You'll find Internet sites that offer creative suggestions for saving money at the end of the chapter. The Reference list at the end of the book includes books about saving money on everyday expenses. Both these lists will show you ways you can save money for investing and not feel deprived while you are doing it.

The Power of Compound Interest

If you are thinking about the belt-tightening you may face in order to get enough cash to begin your rental-purchase plan, it may help to look at the way *compound interest* will help you out. Compounding is the process by which the yearly increase in the value of an investment or of your savings is added back before the next year's increase is calculated. In Chapter 2 you saw that the duplexes Jessica and Caitlin bought increased in value. But we looked at just one year's increase. Now let's see how their investments grow in value if the real estate market in their community continues to grow at seven percent per year.

Over five years, the value of each duplex will increase by more than 40 percent. It hardly seems possible, but, see for yourself:

Year	Value	
1997	$100,000	
1998	107,000	
1999	114,490	
2000	122,504	
2001	131,080	
2002	140,255	**more than 40 percent increase**

If you apply these numbers to the dollars you are going to save for investment, you can see that the sooner you start, the better. But any time is better than never. Start now tucking money away and let the power of compounding help you start your investment plan. You'll be glad you did.

Remind yourself constantly that whatever you choose for an austerity program, it is in a good cause. You are investing in your future. The pain of austerity won't last, and it will be more than offset by your joy in your first purchase.

Summary

✔ Calculate the maximum amount of closing costs you can afford based on your financial picture.

✔ Check with your Realtor to find out a range of fees charged by attorneys in your area for closing. Be sure to add this to your expected costs..

✔ Check to see if cash may be available from your home, your family, or your friends.

✔ Analyze your spending habits to see where you can make savings that will go into your investment account.

✔ Plan for some temporary life-style changes to get your investment plan off the ground.

■ *On the Internet*

Sites with ideas for cutting your living expenses include
www.frugalliving.about.com
www.newdream.org
www.stretcher.com
www.familymoney.com

Want to get cash out of your house? Try these sites
www.nhema.org
www.pueblo.gsa.gov/money

This site will help you monitor your credit
www.consumerinfo.com

To calculate your actual spending and work out a trial budget, try
www.usatoday.com

Chapter 10

Finance Your Purchase: The Loan

Take nothing on its looks; take everything on evidence.
CHARLES DICKENS

Asking for a loan can make your heart pound and your palms sweat. Some of the stress comes from the idea of walking into a bank and asking for what seems like a huge amount of money. Worse yet, you are not only going to talk to a stranger about money, you are going to reveal details about your personal finances. Psychologists tell us that for most people, talking about money is about as hard as talking to the kids about sex. Most of us feel we are about to be judged on our financial habits, and probably pretty harshly. No wonder we're intimidated.

What we don't think about is that banks wouldn't make money if they didn't loan money—and making money is the whole idea of a bank. Some people deposit money into the bank, and the bank pays them interest on their account. Then the bank loans that money to others. By charging the borrower more than it pays the depositor, the bank makes its money. If you and I didn't borrow that money, the bank would go broke. We are actually doing the bank a favor by borrowing money. So, repeat this mantra as you head off to talk to a loan officer, "I'm doing you a favor by borrowing money from you."

Shop 'Til You Drop: Finding a Lender

Since the late 20th Century everyone with cash to spare has wanted to loan money for mortgages. Each lender has an agenda, however, and as a prudent investor you should scrutinize potential lenders just as carefully as the lenders scrutinize you.

You saw in Chapter 9 that the fees charged by a lender can have a major impact on the return from your investment. After you have eliminated some lenders by comparing their interest rates and the length of loans they offer, compare their loan fees. A good way to do this is to prepare a table with the fee categories down the side and the lenders across the top. This table or spreadsheet will let you compare several lenders swiftly. Include the following loan fees on your spreadsheet:

- Application fee
- Appraisal fee
- Credit report fee
- Loan origination fee
- Document preparation
- Environmental review fee
- Processing fees
- Lock-in fee (to guarantee an interest rate)
- Commitment fee

To counter misbehavior by some lenders in the past, Congress enacted laws that require a lender to tell you, in writing, what it will cost you to get a loan. The estimate is called a *good-faith estimate*. If the costs on the estimate are radically different from those you've already discussed with your lender, you should demand an explanation.

Now that you know what you need to know, where do you look?

Who Loans Mortgage Money?

The lending landscape has changed since the time when banks were the only source for mortgage loans. Three major categories of lenders now offer mortgage money, with more trying to get federal approval for real estate loans every day. The major categories of lenders are: the federal government; banks, credit unions, and saving and loan firms; and private parties. These groups have different needs and different requirements for loans.

The Federal Government Two agencies, the Federal Housing Administration (FHA) and the Veteran's Administration (VA), are the primary governmental sources for money for real estate purchases. The FHA doesn't actually lend money, but because FHA guarantees, or insures home mortgages, lenders follow FHA guidelines in making loans. Included in those guidelines are rules about the maximum amount of a loan and the maximum time for payoff. Loan ranges depend on the average home cost in each area, and they change frequently.

■ *FHA Home Loan Limits (Oregon, 1999)*

Number of Units	Standard Loan Amount	High Cost Area Limits
1	$ 78,660	$155,250
2	100,600	198,550
3	121,600	240,000
4	151,150	298,350

Finding a lender who offers FHA-insured loans is worth the hunt. The loans are available for as little as three percent down, providing you agree to live in the property for at least a year. Another advantage of FHA-insured loans is that FHA guidelines for appraisal are strict and thorough. Sellers are often willing to make an extra effort to fix problems noted by FHA appraisers because the deal will not go through until the property meets FHA standards.

Veterans Administration Even more desirable than FHA loans are those guaranteed by the VA. Available only to eligible veterans, these loans may be available for no down payment. VA loans are available for one- to four-unit properties, and loan amounts can go as high as $203,000.

Most lenders have brochures that describe what you need to do to qualify for a VA or FHA loan. The lender you choose may even have a specialist on staff who is experienced in walking borrowers through the ins and outs of these government-guaranteed loans. If you can qualify for one of these loans, it is well worth your time to hunt one down.

Banks, Credit Unions, Savings and Loans Most loans made by banks, credit unions, and savings and loan firms are called *conventional loans*. These are loans not made by the VA or insured by FHA. When you read that the mortgage interest rate has risen or fallen, it is conventional loans that are referred to. They are also the loans you see advertised on TV or in your newspaper. Unfortunately, *conventional* does not mean these loans are all alike. You still have to shop carefully for the best deals.

The first decision you need to make as you shop for a loan is whether you want a *fixed-rate* or an *adjustable-rate mortgage* (ARM). And though the word adjustable may give you a chill, adjustable rates have advantages. The devil is, as usual, in the details. Most conventional mortgage lenders offer both fixed-rate and adjustable-rate mortgages with various interests, points, and *maturities*, or lengths of loan.

Fixed-rate mortgage loans are usually offered at a slightly higher interest rate than adjustable-rate loans. You recall that the bank makes its money by lending money that was deposited by its customers. Obviously they want as high a rate as they can get when they may be locking themselves into a set interest rate for as many as 30 years. If the loan has a fixed interest rate and the prime interest rate goes down, lenders win. If prime interest rates go up, borrowers win.

The interest rate quoted by the bank, the S&L, or the Credit Union reflects their best guess about future interest rates. Since they won't be able to increase the interest on a fixed-rate loan, the lender wants a higher interest for fixed-rate loans. They are willing to take a lower interest rate if they know they'll have the chance to adjust that rate during the life of the loan.

Adjustable-rate mortgages often start at an interest rate below that of the fixed-rate loan. Then, the lender adjusts the rate to reflect the change in the prime rate. Through the life of the loan, the interest rate on the loan will move up or down with the prime rate.

You may notice that mortgage interest rates are lower in areas where the real estate market is really hot. The banks are betting that the property they lend on will sell again shortly, giving them a chance to adjust their rates.

The important questions that you need to ask about an ARM mortgage are:

- How often can it be adjusted?
- How much can it be adjusted?
- What is the maximum rate possible, the life-time cap?

Most ARM loans have a life-time cap on the interest rate. In 2002 people were buying rentals for as little as 5.25 percent interest on ARM loans. If that interest could only be adjusted once a year, only one percent at a time, and the life-time cap is three percent, you can see the total interest will top out at 8.25 percent. When interest rates go back up, they may not stop till they get to 12 or 14 percent, as they did in the late 1970s. At that point, a 8.25 percent loan might be very attractive.

Adjustable-rate mortgages are more complex than fixed-rate loans. Several of the books listed in the references at the end of this book do a good job of explaining the ins and outs of both types of loan. Although an ARM could turn out to be just the right kind of loan for you to finance your purchase, you must be clear about what the cost will be to you in the long term. Do your homework before you sign the documents.

Your Credit Union Your credit union may offer conventional loans—either fixed rate or ARM—for purchase of a rental property.

The terms of the loans—interest rate, maturity, fees, and points— may be quite different from those offered by other mortgage lenders. Credit unions frequently offer really good deals. If you are a member, check out what your credit union offers before you make your final decision. If you are not a member of a credit union and would like to be, call several in your area to see if there is a way you can become a member. Or check into the Self Help Credit Union at (800)966-7353 or info@self-help.org. Becoming a member of a credit union is getting easier all the time.

Private Parties The first private party you should turn to for mortgage money is, as I said earlier, the seller of the property you want to buy. The seller may have an *assumable* loan on the property or may be willing to *finance* your purchase herself.

An assumable loan is one that already exists on the property and can be taken over, assumed, by a new buyer. Assumable loans are becoming less frequent, but they are still out there, mostly on older properties. They are definitely worth looking for.

Land-Sale Contracts A buy-sell contract between you and the seller in which the seller lets you pay off the property over time is called a *land-sale contract*. A land-sale contract is often a creative way for a seller to sell a property that does not appeal to the general population, or for a buyer to purchase a property if she does not qualify for other financing. There are several advantages to both buyer and seller in a land-sale contract.

For you as buyer, with no loan fee, no appraisal, no recording fee, and no points to pay, the closing costs will be greatly reduced. You might be able to purchase a rental for much less cash than might be the case with conventional financing. You may also be able to purchase a rental property even if your credit rating is not the greatest.

For the seller, the land-sale contract means a great deal more money than just the sales price—he gets the interest, too. Not only does the seller get both the principal and the interest, he can negotiate a contract that delivers large chunks of cash at times that minimize his capital gains tax or provide cash when he has the greatest need for it.

All conditions of a land-sale contract are negotiable. Depending on your needs and the seller's needs, the down payment may be minimal, or something other than cash—your second car, for example. The payoff may be straight-line *amortization* (debt payoff by installments), or it may include one or more *balloon* payments, large payments due in one chunk

For example, suppose you purchased a $100,000 rental on a land-sale contract. The contract states that the $100,000, at eight percent interest, will be amortized at 30 years, with the balance due after 15 years. Your mortgage payments to the seller will be $734 each month. At the end of 15 years, you will have paid about $15,000 of the principal, and still owe the seller $85,000 in cash. Most people will refinance a property when a balloon comes due. When you accept balloon-payment financing, you are gambling on what interest rates will be when the balloon comes due.

Land-sale contracts with balloon payments can sometimes help you buy a rental more easily than with conventional financing. However, you must figure the balloon into your plans and be prepared for the inevitable day it comes due. The attorney who draws up the contract will discuss several different ways to deal with a balloon. If she doesn't bring it up, be sure you ask about it. Talk to your financial advisor, too.

In a land-sale contract, the seller is the *mortgagee*, the one who holds the mortgage and the deed. When the contract is paid in full, the deed is transferred to the new owner. As deed holder, the seller continues to be legally responsible for the taxes and other assessments against the property until the deed is transferred.

Obviously, all the little ins and outs usually taken care of by the lender now become the responsibility of the buyer and seller. To be sure all those details are covered and dealt with satisfactorily in the

contract, you *must* use an attorney to draw up a contract that protects both the buyer—you—and the seller.

When I sold my first house on a land-sale contract, my attorney
reminded me that she was hired to play "what if" with me. "What if
the buyer cuts down all the trees, paves the back yard, and trashes
the interior?" she asked. "Then they default and you have to fore-
close. You now have to try to sell a house that has lost value due to
the actions of the previous buyer. You need to have a list of conditions the buyer must maintain for the contract to continue."

Attorneys think of these things, thank goodness. A land-sale
contract can be a valuable instrument for you to use to launch your
investment career, but you need the advice of someone who is
watching out for your interests. Talk to your attorney.

Commercial Loans   If the rental property you are ready to buy is
five units or more, you will need to get a commercial loan, and your
road to financial freedom will be somewhat bumpier. Commercial
lenders generally charge at least two percent more in interest than
residential lenders. They often require more paperwork, both for
the loan and at closing. Commercial loans often require a long-form
appraisal that can cost many times what a residential appraisal does.
Lenders may also insist that you provide rent rolls and income calculations for larger properties. However, for the right property,
you'll be happy to deal with these requirements. Most lenders offer
both residential and commercial loans, with different loan officers
handling the application and processing.

Mortgage Brokers   The advertisements you see in the paper and
on TV are often from *mortgage brokers*, people who will find a mortgage loan for you. Brokers usually have their stable of *underwriters*,
the people whose money you will borrow. For their effort in finding
an underwriter, processing the loan, checking credit, and so on,
many mortgage brokers charge a fee. Sometimes this fee is charged
to the borrower in addition to the loan fee charged by the under-

writer. If that is the case, you should decide if you want to pay for the broker's time, or whether you would rather use the money for closing costs and do your own research to find a lender.

Other mortgage brokers operate the way travel agencies used to—the lender pays their fee. If you can find one of these brokers, you may be able to find well-priced mortgage money without spending large amounts of your time shopping for a lender.

If you can find a mortgage broker who has a large number of loan programs available, just having that person match your needs to a specific program can save you lots of time. In that case, it will be worth your time and money to use a broker.

The Internet is another place to look for financial services. Some people have found mortgage lenders on the net and have been happy with their experience. I still prefer the face-to-face negotiations with a real person when I'm spending large amounts of money.

While you're searching for a lender, start compiling the information the lender will want from you.

How's Your Credit?

Lenders do not want to lose money, and one way they avoid doing so is to ensure that the loans they make will be repaid according to the agreement they've made with the borrower. As a result, lenders want to know as much as possible about you as a borrower.

The first place a lender might check to assess the chances that a loan will be repaid is with all the other lenders you have dealt with in the past. National credit reporting firms collect the data and offer it to lenders, for a fee, of course.

Your prospective lender will review two types of information: your *credit rating*, and a credit report that lists all of your *previous credit* along with your payment history.

Your credit rating is a number called a FICO (Fair Isaac Credit Organization) number calculated by the credit reporting firm. It is based on a formula that includes such items as:

- The number of active credit cards you have.
- The number of months since you got a new credit card.
- Your longest late payment on a loan or credit card.
- The number and dates of inquiries about your credit.

You can check up on your FICO number through the credit reporting Internet site at the end of the chapter.

Your credit report includes everything from real estate loans to credit cards and may fill several sheets of paper. Each entry will show when the credit was established, what the payment amount was, how prompt you were in making payments, and when the charge was paid off. The information is in code, but a legend that lets you read the code is usually on each sheet.

After years of keeping FICO credit scores secret from borrowers, the industry is now making them available. Check your credit score by going to www.Qspace.com or www.myfico.com. Scores range from 300 to 900. You can guess which score you'd rather have.

Once your lender receives your credit information, it will be processed into a credit rating, from **A** for "great credit," to **D** for "You probably don't want to loan money to this person." **A** credit means the applicant has had few or no credit problems within the previous two years. There is no record of the use of a collection agency and no more than two 30-day late payments.

B credit means that there may have been one 90-day late payment and two 60-day late payments and up to four 30-day late payments. Some of these may have been within the previous 18 months.

C credit means that there are numerous 30- to 60-day late payments in the previous two years. It also includes any bankruptcy or foreclosure within the previous 12 months.

If you have any concerns about your credit, or if you just want to know what is in the reports before your lender sees it, you can get a report from one of the credit reporting agencies. Note that I said reports. Several agencies collect credit information. Reports from different agencies often contain different information. Review your credit reports for accuracy and contact the agency to correct any errors you find.

One caveat about checking your own credit report: Each time your credit report is called for, your score may drop several points. This is because the reporting agency assumes an inquiry about your credit means you are getting another credit card or borrowing money. You'd think that if it had your name attached to the request, they could figure out that you weren't the Bank of America, wouldn't you? But the practice means you need to limit your inquiries.

Less Than Sterling Credit? If your credit is less than sterling, there are still ways you can borrow money to buy a rental. The first strategy is to commit to cleaning up your credit and saving and scrounging up enough money to cover your closing costs.

As a second option, you can find a lender willing to make a *sub-prime loan*, a loan made to someone with **C** or **D** grade credit. The lender who makes sub-prime loans is taking a risk that the loan will not be repaid according to the agreement. To cover that risk the lender charges a higher—sometimes a lot higher—interest rate.

Lenders sometimes think of people with poor credit as unsophisticated and unlikely to know when they are being taken advantage of, or unlikely to complain if they do know. As a result, some lenders conduct what regulators call predatory lending practices. These include:

- Charging unacceptably high interest rates.
- Promoting loans in which the principal is never repaid—interest-only loans.
- Padding the closing costs with "junk" fees, those with no purpose beyond making money for the lender.
- Foreclosing on mortgages without due process.
- Changing the numbers on the day of closing without informing the borrower.

If your credit rating is poor enough that you fear that you won't qualify for the usual conventional or FHA loan, you should consider talking to a mortgage broker about sub-prime loans. However, make sure you do your homework and understand exactly how much in closing costs you will be expected to pay. Better yet, plan to wait until you have established good credit before you borrow money to launch your investment career.

The Loan Package

You can find a sample residential real estate loan application on the Internet. You'll see that the lender wants complete information on your financial status including:

- Your financial statement.
- Current bank statements from all banks and credit unions where you have accounts.
- A list of all creditors, along with addresses and account numbers.
- A list of your monthly personal income and expenses subject to verification.
- Two or three year's back tax returns.
- A "gift letter" if a relative is providing a gift of funds to you for your purchase.
- Documentation on alimony and/or child support payments you receive, or pay.
- Current tax statements on the property you are purchasing.

You may also be asked to sign a form giving your permission for the IRS to send a copy of your return to the lender.

Pre-Qualified or Pre-Approved If you have *pre-qualified* for a loan, that means the lender has reviewed your credit and considers you an acceptable risk. *It does not mean the lender has decided to loan you a certain amount.* The approval may depend on the size of loan you ask for, as well as the property you buy. If you have sterling credit and the clear ability to repay a loan even if rents fall, the lender may agree to *pre-approve* you for a loan. Pre-approval means, "Call us up and tell us how much you want. We'll have the money waiting for you at closing."

Read through the sample loan application before you talk to a lender so you will be prepared for the questions you'll be asked. Then ask to be pre-approved for a loan. A seller will often lower the price or make other concessions if he knows you essentially have the money in hand, since it means that the sale can close in days rather than in months. Pre-approval gives you a strong negotiating position.

What to Expect at Closing Your transaction and the papers you will sign are different from the ones the seller will sign. The escrow officer will set appointments at different signing times for each of you. The process, called closing, is straightforward.

The closer will have prepared all the documents for your signature. She will present those documents to you, one at a time, in order, explain what each is for, and indicate where you sign or initial. Some documents are for your lender—your loan agreement, the details of your financing, and the hazard insurance you have placed on the property. Some reiterate your agreement with the seller, contingencies and all. The last set of documents will be those that transfer the title of the property to you and record the title under your name in the public records. If you are a first-time buyer, your Realtor will certainly be at the closing with you.

Following closing, the escrow officer will deposit your certified check to a client trust account. She will then write checks on that account to cover your down payment to the seller, and to make your payments for all the closing costs you have incurred including taxes and insurance. The escrow closer takes care of recording the deed transfer and mails copies of the recorded documents to you and to the seller.

Closing can be an emotional time. Remind yourself that nearly everyone feels some apprehension when they take a big financial step, and don't hesitate to ask all the questions you need to ask. The escrow closer and your Realtor understand that you may be nervous and are there to help you. They want your experience to be a positive one and will work to make it so.

Borrowing money is a part of investing in real estate. If you do your homework, you will find a lender who will meet your requirements. Knowing what to expect when you apply for a loan will save you and your lender time, and you will find the process less stressful when you are prepared. Once you have been through the process, the next time it will be much easier.

Summary

✔ Research the various types of loans and decide which fits your circumstances.

✔ Shop around until you find a lender who offers the terms and services you want.

✔ Check out your credit report before you apply for a loan so you don't get any unpleasant surprises.

✔ Don't use a lender who will not give you a signed good-faith estimate of closing costs.

■ *On the Internet*

Check out your credit rating at these sites

www.equifax.com   **www.experian.com**
www.fairisaace.com   **www.myfico.com**

Try these sites for calculators to help you analyze your debt and loan potential

www.freedebtanalyzer.com   **www.smartmoney.com**
www.moneyhe.p.com

For comparison shopping about loans, try

www.E-loans.com   **www.LoansDirect.com**
www.Quickenloans.com

Part Four
Cashing
Out

Chapter 11 | # Get More Cash Out *of Rentals*

I don't want to make a killing, I just want to make a living.
ANONYMOUS

Rental property is not liquid—it cannot easily be converted to cash. You can't call your broker and say, "I need $10,000 by Monday," and expect to get it, as you can when you hold paper securities. The good news, however, is that while getting cash out of rental properties is more complicated and takes longer than writing a check, there are a number of ways to do so. You can sell a property, or you can use a strategy that allows you to take money out without selling. Let's look first at getting cash out without selling.

Liquefy, Don't Liquidate

By the time you've owned a property four or five years, you will have accumulated significant equity, both from the increase in the market value of the property and by having paid down the mortgage. There are several ways you can convert that equity to cash without selling your property.

Refinance As I write this, interest rates are at a 30-year low. I am refinancing all my properties as a way both to lower my debt service and to get some cash. Here is how my refinancing will work with one of my properties:

I owe $80,000 on an eight-plex worth $230,000. The interest rate on the current loan is 8.9 percent, and the payments, or PITI (principle, interest, taxes, and insurance), are $1,200 per month. I plan to refinance the $80,000 balance and borrow an additional $20,000, using the property as collateral. The lender expects the interest rate to be about 7.5 percent. If I borrow $100,000 (the $80,000 balance, plus an additional $20,000) for 15 years at 7.5 percent, my payment will be around $975 a month, $225 less than it currently is.

If you're not failing now and then, it's a sign you're playing it safe.
WOODY ALLEN

Because the new balance will be below 50 percent of the value of the property, the lender will not require an appraisal. The other loan costs will be added to the loan, so I can clear $20,000 with nothing out of my pocket. Better yet, I won't pay taxes on that cash, and the loan cost will be more than offset by the deductibility of the interest.

Many investors make refinancing a core part of their investment plan. They expect to refinance every few years as a way to generate tax-free cash. This is one way you can provide for those large chunks of cash called for in your own investment plan.

Equity Lines of Credit Similar to refinancing, but more flexible, are equity lines of credit. I talked about the process of obtaining a line of credit in Chapter 9. The process is essentially the same for a rental you own as it is for your personal residence. Since you are still using a piece of property as collateral, you'll have an application, credit check, possible appraisal, and loan fees. There is often a minimum amount allowable and an upper limit that you and the lender agree on. These numbers will be different for a rental than they were for your residence, however, the general idea still applies.

The monthly debt service on an equity line of credit is a minimum amount set by the size of your balance. Most lenders prefer that payments be made by automatic electronic deductions from your account. Since balances change monthly, causing payment amounts to change, automatic payments reduce confusion and ensure that the lender gets the correct payment every month.

Chapter 9 listed some of the variables you need to compare to find your best equity line of credit. Here is a more complete list. Use it to rank and compare lenders.

Basic Features

Fixed interest rate

Variable interest rate

Frequency of interest rate adjustments

Interest rate cap

Length of Plan

Draw period

Repayment period

Closing Costs

Application fee

Appraisal fee

Processing fees and points

Other closing costs

Repayment Terms During the Draw Period

Interest and principal payments

Interest only payments

Fully amortizing payments

At the End of the Draw Period

Balloon payment?

Availability of renewal

Balance refinancing by lender?

Equity lines of credit have many advantages. Most have low interest, the cash is usually accessible by check, the interest is tax deductible, and again, you don't pay taxes on the cash you take out. An equity line of credit may be the right way for you to pull money out of your rentals to meet the needs of your financial plan.

Why Sell?

Barring a financial crisis, your reasons for selling a rental property will reflect your financial plan and your investment strategies. As with the rest of your investment plan, your reasons change with your circumstances, such as your age and family considerations.

Aggressive-Growth Selling Strategies One reason you might decide to sell a property is to generate cash to buy more rentals or larger rental complexes. There are two strategies for selling your rental as a way to generate cash for another purchase. One is to sell it outright and pay the capital gains tax. The other strategy is to use a selling process that allows you to defer the tax until some future time—the tax-deferred exchange.

Younger investors, those getting started, and those who want rapid growth in a supportive market, may want to use the *1031 Tax-Deferred Exchange* sales strategy to boot-strap themselves into larger real estate holdings. The tax-deferred exchange allows you to sell an *investment* property, purchase a replacement *investment* property, and defer the tax on the gain from the sale.

Selling a property through an exchange may work best in a stagnant market. Because you must both buy a property and sell a property, you will be most successful in a market that is not terribly volatile. And it is important to remember that the tax you deferred is still there waiting to be paid. The specifics of exchanges are described more fully in the How to Sell section below.

In a rising market you may find that your equity has grown enough to allow you to sell one property and pay the capital gains tax, rather than defer it, and purchase a replacement property. The advantage of this approach is that the tax is paid, and the tax liability will not be attached to your new property.

The thought that a larger asset will include a larger debt service and a larger loan balance may still be intimidating to you. Let's review the advantages of owning larger rentals—complexes with more than four units, so you can see that working your way into larger complexes is not as risky as it might sound.

If your market is growing at ten percent per year, the value of your property will double in just over seven years. The duplex that was worth $100,000 when you bought it will be worth $200,000 in seven years. The $100,000 appreciation represents money in the bank, ready for you to use to advance your investment plan.

If you sell the first duplex on an exchange and roll that money into a $200,000 four-plex, your debt service will be only slightly larger than it was on the original duplex, and the rent will have doubled—you now have four tenants sending you monthly checks, instead of two. If you made a similar exchange seven years later, you might find yourself owning an eight-unit apartment building and collecting rent from eight tenants. Your cash flow and your net worth would have grown substantially; larger assets produce larger gains.

Steady-Income Selling Strategies Aggressive growth may not be the best strategy for you. If your goal is an investment that produces steady cash flow, you could sell the property and carry the contract. Using the example of the $100,000 duplex again, once it is worth $200,000, you might choose to sell it on a land-sale contract. The buyer will pay off your loan balance and owe you the remaining $100,000 or so, along with the interest.

Because the IRS calls this kind of sale an *installment* sale, one where you did not take the entire equity in cash, you will be taxed two ways. The portion of the principal paid off each year will be taxed at your marginal rate as capital gains. The interest you receive each month, a much larger amount, will be taxed at your standard rate. Eventually, when the entire contract is paid off, you'll find you have paid much less in capital-gains tax because the gain came to you in small installments.

Most installment sales include a balloon payment—often the balance on the contract. You could, however, arrange a series of balloons. You can time balloon payments for periods when your capital gains tax will be less of a burden than it might otherwise be. Or you can time the balloon payment(s) to meet other obligations, such as college tuition or vacation trips. If your need for cash can be predicted, you can write the timing into the contract.

The U.S. Tax Code is complicated, and you should confer with your team members before you sell a property. Your attorney and your tax person will help you design strategies to help you toward your financial goals while minimizing the tax impact. Talk to them before you sell.

When to Sell

One characteristic real estate investing shares with stand-up comedy is the importance of timing. People in a position to invest in a rapidly rising market make money—lots of it—in a hurry. Those who are forced to sell in a sagging market, either don't make what they had hoped, or they lose money.

Realtors like to say, "Your money is made when you buy real estate, not when you sell," meaning that if you buy under conditions that are not favorable to you, you will never make the money you had counted on. Either you will have to hold the property longer than you wanted, or you will be forced to sell in less than favorable conditions.

Unfortunately, predicting the real estate market is not an exact science. Real estate markets may be easier to predict than the stock market, but there are still variables you can't control. For example, when the Federal Reserve Board pretended to see inflation lurking just around the corner in the spring of 1994 and raised interest rates, the market in my area dropped 30 percent in about ten days. All over town Realtors and mortgage lenders were looking as if they had just walked into a moving bus. If you had planned to sell in a depressed market like that, your plans would have needed sudden and extreme adjustment.

The good news was that the market rebounded within a few months. People still needed someplace to live, and rental properties were still saleable. The way to protect yourself against these kinds of sudden changes in the market is to recognize that they happen. The most important thing any investor learns is that all business is cyclic. Remember that the idea that helped fuel the "bubble" of the 1990s was the idea that business had changed and we were living in a "New Paradigm" with no cycles. Turns out there was nothing new about it, and the cycles reappeared.

Yearly Cycles in Real Estate Barring sudden changes, like big jumps in interest rates, your study of your local market should allow you to watch the cycles, some of which are yearly.

A caution about watching markets is that the market cycle is not the same for all classes of properties. The yearly cycle affects single-family home market more than it does the market for small multiplexes. Because duplexes and four-plexes are intermediate between single-family homes and large apartment buildings, the small multiplex market will share similarities with both single-family and commercial real estate.

The people who buy single-family homes are usually single families, not investors. Few families want to move over the holidays, during the winter, or just after school has started. Sales of single-family homes pick up in March and April as buyers expect 30- to 60-day waits for closing and occupancy. This same 30- to 60-day lag is apparent at the send of summer; sales drop off about the first of July, and the market begins to sag about the time the kids are ready to go back to school.

Your best selling strategy might be to put a duplex on the

market in about March or April when your units are most fully occupied. If you are buying, you might want to be prepared to purchase in late January or early February, when the market is slow and prices at their lowest. Obviously, that may conflict with selling on a tax-deferred exchange, because of the time limits. Be sure to talk to your consultants about your scheduling.

Attitude Adjustment for Stress Reduction My local market took off in late 1993. I now shake my head about selling a single-family house in 1992 for $86,000. I have no doubt it would have brought $130,000 by mid-1994. But I vowed early on that I wasn't going to cry over things like that. I nearly doubled my equity in the property as it was, and I was able to roll it into a duplex in a transaction that lowered my mortgage payments and doubled the rent. My cash flow went from $30 per month to $400 per month with that transaction.

Yes, that additional $45,000 would have been nice to play with. But my financial plan called for moving out of the single-family units into multiplexes. I believe the transaction improved my position significantly, and as long as that was the case, I didn't try to second guess the market or myself. There is a real danger with holding a property too long just because you believe the market will improve. Give yourself permission to do "reasonably well." Remember, you are investing to make a living, not a killing.

How to Sell

Your decisions about how to sell depend on your reasons for selling. If you want aggressive growth in your portfolio, then you will want to consider a 1031 exchange. If you want an income stream, you will be thinking about installment sales. Another strategy for income stream might be to consider transactions that will remove or reduce debt on one or more properties. You might sell one duplex and pay off the mortgage on the other. Then all the net income from the second duplex is yours—minus expenses, of course.

The 1031 Tax-Deferred Exchange: The Details The IRS will allow you to defer the capital gains tax on the sale of income property if you use the proceeds to purchase another piece of income property. The tax liability is carried forward onto the new piece of property.

For a transaction to qualify for tax-deferred status, the property you sell and the property you buy must both be investment properties. There is some question about whether the property must actually produce income.

The purchase price of the new property must be equal to, or higher than, the selling price of the old one. And the equity in the new property must be equal to, or higher than, the equity in the old one. The shorthand Realtors use for the rule is, "like for like, and even or up."

If the equal or higher criteria for purchase price and equity are not met, you will pay tax on the difference. Sometimes, however, the tax is actually smaller than a year's worth of interest on a larger loan. Don't structure a transaction simply to avoid all tax. Do the numbers. Both tax and penalties, if any, may be less than the first year's interest on the larger loan.

Very seldom will you find a property you want to buy at exactly the same moment a buyer makes an offer on your property, so you usually won't be able to do simultaneous exchanges. That timing problem prompted Congress to adopt the *Starker Exchange Rules.*

Starker rules give you 45 days from the closing time of your sale to *identify* a replacement property that qualifies for exchange benefits. Since the process of qualifying is open to interpretation, most exchange advisors recommend that you be ready to sign an earnest money agreement within 45 days of closing on the sold property.

You may see real estate ads that tell you a prospective buyer or seller wants the transaction for a 1031 exchange. Often the person is coming close to the end of the 45-day period and sees a large tax bill looming on the horizon.

Obviously the timing issue can be a problem. There may not be a property available for you to buy when you're ready for an exchange. It may not be a good idea to sell if there is little on the market that interests you. Or, if you have an opportunity to sell for a good price, you might buy a less-than-perfect replacement property and sell it when something you really want becomes available. Realtors call this "parking the proceeds."

Seller Financing   After years of maintaining rental properties and dealing with renters, selling on a contract can make it seem that you have arrived in Nirvana. Every month the escrow company sends you a nice check. At the end of the year, it sends a statement that can be transferred directly to your tax form, all without the headaches of management. If your goals call for converting some of your properties into a regular income stream, this may be the strategy for you.

In tight money markets or soft real estate markets, seller financing may be the only way to sell a property. The buyer has to qualify only in your opinion and your attorney's. And you set the interest rate, which may be below the going rate.

Selling on a contract does have its pitfalls. Be sure to have your attorney, an expert on real estate transactions, draw up the contract. As you might guess, you have much more at risk when you carry the contract. In a land-sale contract sale, you hold the title to the property until the last payment is made.

Remember the earlier example? The buyers take possession of your property and promptly let it fall apart. No one does any yard work. The plumbing leaks are not fixed, the roof is not repaired or replaced, and the interior is trashed. Now suppose that this goes on for five years, at which time the buyer skips town and leaves no forwarding address. You will get the property back, because you still own it. But you now have the legal cost of foreclosure, and the cost of rehabilitating the property before you can put it back on the market.

Because on a seller-held contract you own the property until it's paid for, you will need to protect against such scenarios as the one above. Here are some suggestions:

- Get a credit report on the buyer. Make sure you are comfortable with the report.

- Require—in writing—that the buyer buy and maintain a homeowner's insurance policy. A catastrophic fire could eliminate your source of income.

- Be sure to include in the contract the requirement that the buyer make timely tax payments. Then, invest in tax registration coverage, a form of insurance that alerts you if the property taxes are not paid. The coverage is offered by title insurance companies.

- Include a contingency that requires that the buyers must notify you if they plan to sell and that you must approve a new buyer.

- Be sure to insist that the payments be handled through an escrow company. Buyers are less likely to call an escrow company with excuses about late payments and arguments about late-payment fees. Your peace of mind will be well worth the small fee charged for collection.

After the sale you might even want to conduct monthly drive-by inspections and yearly inspections inside the unit(s).

Seller financing is an excellent alternative in tight markets or to meet a specific investment strategy. But the process is complicated and full of potential problems. A detailed discussion is outside the scope of this introductory book.

Rental properties do not provide large amounts of ready cash as easily as some paper investments. You can't sell off the garage or a bedroom for quick cash. In order to get cash, beyond your normal cash flow from your rentals, you will need to plan a process that meshes with your investment strategies and your financial circumstances. Think about the possibilities and work them into your investment plan.

Summary

✔ The process of getting large amounts of money out of rental properties is more complex and slower than for some other investments.

✔ You don't have to sell to get large infusions of cash from your rentals.

✔ If you do plan to sell, there are several strategies to explore, including equity lines of credit and refinancing.

■ *On the Internet*

Use the same calculators that you used in Chapter 6 to find out how much your equity is worth:

www.nhema.org

www.pueblo.gsa.gov/money.

www.bankrate.com

Part Five:
How
to Be a
Landowner

Chapter 12

Manage
Your Rental
Business

It's All in the Details

If a window of opportunity opens, don't pull down the shade.
TOM PETERS

You should approach your investments as a business, because they *are* a business—just as a mail-order catalog run out of your garage is a business. The IRS will treat you like a business owner, so from the very beginning of your career in rentals you should be as businesslike as possible

Those Pesky Details

If your first rental investment is a single-family home or a duplex, you should think about managing it yourself. Even if you soon hire a management firm, you need to know what kind of decisions must be made, what sort of record keeping is useful and required, and what your tolerance is for the details of property management.

My management firm keeps records, inspects properties, screens new tenants, collects and records rents, produces monthly statements, and evicts troublesome tenants. I doubt that I'd be as thankful for my managers as I am if I hadn't done the job myself for a couple of years.

Whether you choose to manage your own properties or to have someone else do it for you, you'll have to put in some minimal amount of time making sure the details of your investments run smoothly. As the owner, you will be the person ultimately responsible, whether it is to your own financial goals, to the IRS, or to a tenant who believes she has a damage claim. I get a lot of enjoyment from keeping track of my properties, and I think you will too.

Record Keeping Professional management can take a great deal of the pain of record keeping from your shoulders. A good manager will provide you with detailed monthly statements showing income and expense for each property. Most management firms attach copies of the invoices from providers of goods and services to the statement, so you can verify the numbers monthly. A good manager will be happy to discuss any concerns you have about any of the numbers. Be suspicious of managers who don't want to discuss finances with you.

Each monthly statement, whether you or the manager generated it, should include a *year-to-date* (YTD) column. This column is especially valuable on your December 31st statement, since it covers the entire previous year. From that statement, you can transfer the YTD numbers directly to your tax schedule.

Monthly operating statements for your rentals allow you to see directly how each property is performing. Going over the statements gives you the opportunity to apply the valuation techniques you learned when looking for property. You can enter the income and expenses for your properties into the formulas and calculate your cash flow. And you can use your knowledge of your market to convert from your NOI through several possible cap rates to calculate possible market values of your properties.

For your own tracking purposes you may want to develop a spreadsheet of your *schedule of real estate owned*, showing all the details you want to track. On mine, I include original cost, current balance, gross rents, PITI payments, account numbers, and a place for comments. Use your monthly statements to update your spreadsheet at least quarterly. Keeping your spreadsheet up to date gives you current information for loan applications. And it is rewarding to look at the numbers each quarter and realize how your investments are increasing in value.

The Facets of Rental Management If you decide to manage your own rentals, you will have three major components to attend to: managing the finances, managing the tenants, and managing the property.

Managing Your Finances

The first thing you'll need to do, both to simplify your life and to make the IRS happy, is to establish a separate bank account for all transactions having to do with your investments. You should put all rents and deposits into this account and write all expense checks from it.

A professional management firm uses a *client trust account* (a non-interest-bearing account) for all transactions having to do with the rentals they manage. This account is separate from the one they use for their standard office expenses, such as salaries and supplies. You need to operate essentially the same way. Keep your business money separate from your personal money. Mixing business money and personal money is called *co-mingling*, and it is severely frowned on by the IRS and by most state regulators.

Managing Your Tenants

If you decide to manage your first property yourself, you may find, as I did, that the hardest work is managing tenants. I learned it was not what I wanted to do with my time. You may thrive on it.

Tenant Selection Just as buying the right property largely determines the success of an investment, selecting the right tenant determines the success of the landlord-tenant relationship. The cost of evicting a bad tenant, trying to collect on bounced checks, and cleaning up a trashed property makes the time and effort invested in selecting the right tenant seem like money well spent.

Looking at properties from the point of view of a renter—asking yourself about convenience, safety, and appeal—will help you chose properties people will be eager to rent. However, it may also make you vulnerable to smooth talkers. You need to be able to move between the two points of view.

Remind yourself you are running a business. You may be attempting to increase the inventory of affordable housing in your community, but you can't do that if you are driven out of business by poor tenant selection. Set your standards, put them in writing, and don't deviate.

Credit Checks Once you have established yourself as a business person with a business checking account, you can ask for a credit check on your rental applicants. Credit checks cost money. Find out what you'll be paying for tenant screening and charge a non-refundable application fee to cover the cost of the credit investigation. Websites and phone numbers for the major credit reporting firms are found at the end of the chapter.

References I learned the hard way that other landlords aren't always the best sources for references. If the current landlord wants to get rid of a tenant, he is hardly going to tell you about all his faults. Rather, he's going to tell you this tenant is a great guy and hope you can't hear him saying to himself, "Please take this jerk off my hands."

Professional management services, on the other hand, will probably give you a good assessment of tenant performance. Be sure to ask if they would be willing to rent to the person again.

What else should you ask? Make yourself a list of questions and be sure you ask all of them each time you check references. You want to know if the tenant paid the rent on time, if he kept the premises maintained, if he was the source of complaints from neighbors. That is, did the renter fulfill the terms of the rental agreement?

Operating from a standard set of questions for both tenants and references will forestall accusations of bias. If you can prove that you ask everyone the same questions, you can show that no person has been singled out for special treatment.

Rental Agreements Rental agreements are the way you communicate your expectations to the prospective tenant. In this document you outline exactly what you are providing and what you expect in return. You can usually find rental contracts from such organizations as Stevens Ness at larger office supply stores. Most rental-owner organizations provide forms to their members, for a fee. Forms produced by these organizations often reflect local conditions better than generic forms you can buy elsewhere.

Tenant Relations The happiest and most successful landlords seem to be those who get the tenant on their side. There are several ways to do this. One is to offer the tenant a discount on rent if she agrees to handle small maintenance problems on her own. This allows the landlord to escape the nagging telephone calls and gives the tenant some responsibility for the maintenance of the unit, as well as a small reward for taking that responsibility.

A creative technique used by a local rental owner is to run a monthly competition for the most attractive yard. The winner gets one month free rent. This manager controls several square blocks of tidy duplexes. As you can imagine, the contest produces a very attractive, well- maintained neighborhood. He can charge some of the highest rents in the area—and get them—and renters feel they have a chance to win big.

In larger metropolitan areas, some management firms are diversifying by offering specific help to owner-managers on a contract basis. For example, one manager in my area offers to do evictions, from start to finish, for a set fee. Given the time-consuming nature of the eviction process and the need for extensive knowledge, I consider his service a bargain. There are probably similar services in your area.

Managing Your Property

The demands of the physical upkeep of rental properties is one of the first things people mention when they share their fears of owning rentals. The problems involved with maintenance of a property will be reduced if you have the skills to do much of the work yourself, or the skill and experience to supervise subcontractors to do the work for you.

Along with the skill to supervise maintenance work, you need to have a stable of repair workers, electricians, plumbers, and flooring installers lined up to respond when you need them. If you plan to manage your property yourself, you should find as many names of reliable workers in these trades as you can before you buy your first property. Chapter 14 describes ways to find these workers and to work with them.

Rental-Owner Associations   The biggest help to you in your beginning efforts to learn the property-management business may be your local rental-owner association. Among the services you'll find at such an association are guest speakers on most phases of rental management such as tenant screening, credit checking, and evictions. My local organization recently had a speaker from EPA talking about the new regulations governing lead-based paints.

Many rental-owner associations provide well-designed forms for purchase and use by members. The array of forms, rental applications, lease agreements, late payment and eviction notices, are the culmination of years of experience. The forms cover most contingencies and have been reviewed by an attorney. Rental association forms will be worth your time to investigate.

Summary

✔ If you plan to manage your rentals yourself, establish a business checking account.

✔ Set up a process for keeping accurate financial records for your rental properties as soon as you buy your first property.

✔ Develop a written process for selecting tenants. Don't deviate from it.

✔ Use printed forms from your local rental management organization for tenant screening, rental agreements, and other routine operations.

✔ If you plan to use a management organization, be sure to interview several to find the one that best meets your needs.

Chapter 13 |

Fix Up
for Fun
and Profit

Use it up, wear it out. Make it do, or do without.
ANONYMOUS

Preserving older buildings maintains the character of a neighborhood and the history of a community. Rehabbing existing properties, rather than razing them and rebuilding, reduces the drain on natural resources and provides an outlet for your creative drive.

Buying fixer-upper properties and rejuvenating them to rent or to sell can also increase your cash flow and your net worth. Buyers and renters both respond to the appearance of a property, and both will pay more for attractive properties. If you have the skills and inclination, you may be able to purchase a property at a reasonable price and use your time and effort to increase both its sales value and the rents it commands.

By skills I don't mean you need to be a building contractor. A fresh coat of exterior paint can increase the price of a house as well as the speed with which it sells. Freshly painted walls, new carpets, and new vinyl in kitchen and bath will increase rents and tenant satisfaction. And almost anyone can paint an interior.

What It Takes: The Fixer Mindset

In order to make a renovation project pay off, you'll need to do a lot of the work yourself. The money you would pay a contractor to paint the interior of a house, for example, may be a large part of the profit you were counting on at sale. In order to profit from your investment, you'll have to pay yourself that money, instead of a contractor.

You need to enjoy at least some of the fixing-up process. No amount of money is worth sweating away at a job you hate. You will take longer and do a poorer job if you don't like doing it. Your time is almost always better spent doing something you like to do. Here are some questions to ask yourself before you consider fixing up properties for investment:

- Do you repaint your bedroom every couple of years just because you want to change the color?
- Do you suspect there is no real mystery to what makes a house tick, even if you don't know all about it right now?
- Do you believe you can learn most things if you put your mind to it?
- Are you reasonably good with your hands—do you sew or do crafts?
- Does your family ask you to wrap the birthday and Christmas gifts?
- Do you tolerate surprises reasonably well?

If you answered *yes* to most of these questions, you probably have the skills and attitudes necessary to be a successful fixer-upper.

As a beginning fixer-upper, you'll need expert support and advice as you learn to use the materials and equipment of the trade. That advice is easier to obtain than you might think. Don't be afraid to ask the contractors you know how to do particular jobs. Ask clerks at the supply stores for demonstrations and advice. The salespeople at the paint store, for example, have extensive experience with their products and supplies and will be happy to demonstrate them for you. Building supply stores and the big do-it-yourself centers run demonstrations on most weekends. Ask, and ask, and ask.

One caution about the previous advice. Large department stores that just happen to have a paint or hardware department are seldom good places to get help. Clerks in these stores may rotate positions frequently. They are often not trained in the use and application of specific tools and materials.

Look to the specialty stores for help, and be sure to ask if you qualify for contractor discounts as a rental owner. Many venders will be happy to oblige, and will be willing to open a charge account for you as well. If you have a number of units, a monthly billing from a supplier can simplify your bookkeeping.

For learning on your own, you can't beat the do-it-yourself books by Sunset, Ortho, and 3M. These books use clear, step-by-step instructions and detailed pictures on projects from home wiring to window coverings. The books are available at your bookstore, at the do-it-yourself stores, and at libraries. Even in instances where you're not going to do the work yourself, these books can explain building and maintenance to you and help you learn how it all works.

The first Sunset book I bought was *Walks, Walls and Patio Floors*. Under its guidance I excavated and poured a 16-by-24-foot patio. I did find a friend who could supervise the actual concrete pouring. But I calculated the amount of cement necessary, built the forms, laid the rebar, and called the cement company—all from the instructions in the book. I was incredibly proud of that patio. I decided I could do brain surgery if I could find the right Sunset book.

Colleges and community colleges in your area may teach classes in home repair or remodeling. The teachers in these classes are usually professionals. You will learn more, and faster, taking a class from an experienced craftsperson than you will from your own spotty experiences. Take a look at the catalog of a college near you.

Buy good equipment and good products. Until you experience it, you won't believe the difference you'll find in applying a good grade of paint compared to a poor quality product. Good paint flows on, covers well, and is easy to clean up. Poor paint makes the roller feel as if it's sticking to the wall.

One of my contractors told me to buy a better grade of sheetrock mud after he listened to me whine about my sloppy seams. Sheetrock mud is the stuff used to cover seams between sheets of dry wall. He also suggested thinning the mud with water to a whipped cream consistency. I couldn't believe the difference his suggestions made. I still get mud in my hair, but my seams no longer look as if they were done by a three-year-old. Little tricks of the trade can make all the difference, and contractors usually like to share them.

How to Find the Right Fixer

Notice I haven't mentioned your inclinations toward electrical work or plumbing. You want your first fixer-upper to be one that doesn't need much of that very expensive work. The most profitable fixer-uppers are those that need painting inside and out, landscaping, new light fixtures, window coverings, and new carpeting. You might call this work redecorating; Realtors call it *cosmetic work*.

Cosmetic work changes the appearance of the property, and you can manage most of it, even if you are a beginner. Surprisingly, interior painting and papering are often very expensive if you have to hire someone to do them. All in all, they are great projects for the amateur.

Selecting a property that needs largely cosmetic work requires a careful inspection. Consider adding a contractor or a structural engineer to your team when you are looking for fixer-uppers. You may want their advice to make sure there are no large structural, mechanical, or electrical problems.

Structural Considerations The structural areas that need the most careful inspection are at the top and bottom of the building: the roof, the floors, and the foundation. An inspector will usually evaluate the roof in terms of its remaining life. You'll be told the roof has three years remaining, for example, or 15 years. Often a local roofer will do an inspection for a small fee, hoping to be hired to replace the roof if replacement is needed. Since this produces a bit of a conflict of interest, you may want to leave the roof inspection in the hands of the whole-house inspector.

On the bottom of the building, the floors, you'll need to know how much dry rot there is around water sources such as sinks, tubs, and toilets. Most fixer-uppers are bound to have some dry rot; you need to know how much there is and what it might cost to fix.

Dry-rot repairs can run into thousands of dollars if the rot has gone through the floor and into the supporting beams, requiring repair to underlying structures. At the very least, a dry-rot repair means new vinyl flooring for the room. Because this is work best done by experts, it can be the most expensive part of a fix-up. But you may find that a particular purchase is still a good deal financially. What you need to avoid is the serious structural repair problem. Your whole-house inspector will give you an estimate of the extent of the damage and the cost to repair.

Cracked or missing foundations often turn out to be easily repaired. You need to discuss these structural issues with a builder or an engineer before you decide to purchase a building with foundation problems. But don't just automatically avoid buildings with foundation issues.

The mechanical systems you'll need to have inspected are the electrical system, the plumbing, and the heating and cooling systems. These inspections are difficult to do yourself, and the potential cost of repair or replacement of these systems is enormous. The expense is nearly always well beyond the return you would hope to make on resale or the increased rent you might command.

Many state building codes will not allow an owner to do plumbing, electrical, or structural repair on buildings that will be rented to others. State laws require that these repairs be done by licensed, state-certified contractors. Local building permit processes also require that such repairs be inspected and approved by the appropriate building inspector. Permits and code inspections are time-consuming and expensive, and best avoided if you can—stick to cosmetics at first.

When inspecting a fixer-upper, you need to separate the possible fix-and-sell property, called a *flipper* in the trade, from the property you will buy and hold to rent. For example, if the building has cracks in the foundation, finding the cause and repairing the foundation will increase the price on resale. A renter, however, won't pay more rent just because the foundation has been repaired.

A renter might pay more for fresh paint and new carpet. But a buyer will often ask for a discount on the price instead. New buyers usually want to pick their own colors and would prefer that decorating be left to them.

The Cost of Supplies My property manager says the things that allow her to increase the rent are new paint, new window coverings, new carpeting and vinyl, and remodeled kitchens and baths. The most expensive items are the kitchen and bath cabinetry, followed by carpeting. An efficient use of your time before you actually find your fixer-upper will be to locate sources of *inexpensive* materials and labor. Inexpensive means low cost, not low quality.

Here are some ways to save money on upgrading a property without sacrificing quality.

Vinyl flooring Unless you have experience installing sheet goods, use self-sticking vinyl tiles. You should be able to find these for $4.50 a yard or less at do-it-yourself outlets. Many rental owners are beginning to use snap-together laminate flooring.

Carpeting As a rental property owner you should be able to find a supplier willing to give you a special price on carpeting. Your rental-owner association may have some deals worked out with suppliers, and members will have good advice Ask your local property managers for names of good suppliers and installers. Lots of professional carpet and vinyl installers moonlight during the evening and on weekends doing installations for private parties.

Kitchen/Bath Cabinetry If the cabinetry is beyond restoration with a quick paint job, you may need to replace it. Building-supply stores now carry lines of assemble-them-yourself cabinets, called "knock-down" (KD) in the trade. They are easy to assemble with only a hammer, screw driver, and bottle of white glue. KD cabinetry can cost less than half what custom cabinetry does.

One caution, a box of KD cabinetry is unbelievably heavy. I have the store load the boxes in my truck or station wagon. Then I slit the carton, carefully, with a box knife, and slide the pieces out one at a time to carry inside to assemble. I try to put them together where they will be used. When they are assembled, I can slide them into place and never have to actually pick one up.

Another solution to seriously damaged cabinetry is to replace just the doors. Most building-supply stores can order custom doors. When these doors are painted to match the existing frames the effect is that of a new kitchen. This solution is more expensive than the knocked-down cabinets. But with badly damaged cabinetry, it may be the only one, short of entirely new cabinets.

Counter Tops Building-supply stores have pre-formed (often called post-formed) counter tops available in standard lengths. Prefab counter tops can cost as little as $4 a linear foot, which makes your kitchen counter cost just $32 for an 8-foot counter, rather than $400 to $800 for a professionally installed counter. You can use post-formed counter-tops on bath vanities too.

A second option for do-it-yourself counter tops is ceramic tile.

Tile installation is surprisingly easy, and it is one of the most expensive jobs if you have to pay someone else to do it. Tile counters lift any kitchen or bath out of the ordinary.

Paint and Wallpaper   The biggest surfaces in a room, hence the most noticeable, are the walls, followed by the floors. Use high-grade paint on walls; it covers well, is easy to maintain, and looks better than bottom-of-the-line products.

Decide on a basic color—some shade of white wears best—then use that color consistently. That way you won't stand there scratching your head wondering just what color is on that wall when it's time to touch up. Store extra paint in a heated area, or don't buy much of it at a time, because latex paint is ruined if it freezes.

Wallpapers can jazz up any room, but they are easier to damage and harder to repair than painted surfaces. I like to use wallpaper borders up next to the ceiling. They still add sparkle and they're up out of harm's way.

Another place to use wallpaper is on walls or ceilings with cracks and nicks that would be expensive and time-consuming to repair. Several lines of thick, highly textured papers are available that can conceal all these flaws. The papers can be painted and look like plastered walls when finished. These papers also work well to cover old paneled walls.

Miniblinds   Miniblinds provide an attractive, lower-cost option to draperies, which are easily damaged and expensive to clean and repair. Blinds are easy to install, available in a wide range of sizes and colors, and cost about a tenth of what drapes for most windows cost. If your decorator soul demands an accent color, you can add a bright valance and still spend less money than you would on drapes.

Appliance Paints   Older rental units often contain avocado fridges, harvest gold ranges, yellow dishwasher fronts, and copper-colored hoods. Appliance refinishing can make all those appliances the same color—any color you wish. An electrostatic coating process lets appliances be refinished right in the kitchen with the color you choose. The finished product has the look, feel, and surface durability of a new appliance. For what you get, it is usually very reasonably priced. Look for appliance refinishing in the yellow pages.

I've put all these strategies to work at one time or another. The one I'm proudest of is using KD cabinetry to add to a kitchen that had old, solid-plywood cabinets. I painted the new cabinets and the old ones the same color and used the same pulls on them. The kitchen looks as if it has custom cabinetry.

I added a butcher-block island to one kitchen for about $200, instead of the nearly $1000 it would have cost to do it the usual way. I painted a KD base cabinet to match the rest of the kitchen, then topped it with an oiled butcher-block top that was actually the top of an unfinished computer desk. A supplier in my area makes these desks out of hardwood scraps, glued and milled so they look like butcher-block.

The Danger of Fixing Up

If you've done some redecorating in your own home, you know the hazard of painting the walls. Suddenly the counter tops look outdated, the appliances mismatched, and the curtains worn. You will have the same response to a newly painted room in your investment property, and it may make sense to continue upgrading. But now you're a business person. Be alert to the possibility of over-improving a property. Continue only if it makes financial sense. Be sure your upgrades will increase either the rents or the market value or both.

Environmental Hazards

As owner of commercial property you need to know a little about environmental issues: the possibility of lead in the old paint you want to scrape off, the presence of asbestos in the stuff covering the heating ducts, and the presence of underground tanks for fuel storage. You don't need to be an expert on any of these problems; the experts are available for you to consult. But you do need to know about the possibilities, when to ask questions, and when to go slow.

Most buildings constructed before 1978 are assumed to be possible sources of lead paints. Many of the fixer-uppers you'll look at will fall into this category. Be sure to obtain a copy of the lead-based-paint regulations from your realtor before you attack the woodwork with a sander and fill the air with lead-contaminated dust.

Many cities are enforcing environmental regulations more than ever. It is possible to have your entire remodeling operation shut down if an inspector discovers that you are scraping off lead-based paint or asbestos-laden floor tiles without proper precautions. Ask your local rental-owner association about regulations in your area, then pay a consultant to keep you out of trouble.

Fixing up distressed properties can make sense financially and environmentally. Be sure to figure out if you have the stamina and mind set necessary to do the work before you buy a fixer. Then line up your consultants and get ready to have fun turning that sow's ear into a silk purse.

Summary

✔ Fixing up distressed properties is good for your community, your bottom line, and your creative streak.

✔ Decide how much time, energy, skill, and perseverance you have before you buy a fixer-upper.

✔ Locate sources of information—contractors, friends, building-supply stores—before you start.

✔ Unless you have strong construction skills, limit yourself to cosmetic fixing the first couple of times.

✔ Be sure to have potential purchases inspected thoroughly before you buy.

✔ Locate sources of high-quality, low-cost materials before you start your project.

✔ Be conscious of possible environmental hazards in all projects.

■ *On the Internet*

www.tjbhomes.com

www.resourceventure.org

www.turi.org

www.housingzone.com/topics/green

Chapter 14 | # When You Can't Do It Yourself

Then he nailed right through the conduit, and out went all the lights.

FLANDERS AND SWANN

At some point in your fixing-up career, you are sure to need skilled building help. Whether it is laying carpet, repairing dry-rot damage in the bathroom, or adding electrical outlets, a remodeling chore will come up that you can't—or don't want to—do yourself.

The Ins and Outs of Hiring a Contractor

Unfortunately, few topics are guaranteed to keep the cocktail party conversation going quite as well as the trials of working with contractors. The three big issues with contractors are cost, scheduling, and quality of work. Of course, what other issues are there with remodeling work?

Your state will have some sort of builder-certification board that maintains a file of complaints against contractors, information that will help you when screening potential help. The building permit office in your city will have telephone numbers for the state office. Be sure to check out a potential contractor with the certification board before you hire him or her. You want your contractor to be licensed and bonded, and to have a record free of complaints.

You must also understand the *construction lien* process in your state. A construction lien allows the contractor to hold your property hostage until his bills are paid. A lien clouds your title to the property and makes it impossible to sell or refinance.

> *The only way of discovering the limits of the possible is to venture a little way past them into the impossible.*
> ARTHUR C. CLARKE

Many states require a contractor to give the property owner a signed notice of the right to lien before he starts the work. Supposedly his neglecting to do this negates his right to place a lien on your property and may subject him to a fine. Different states have different statutes, and your contractor board will send you information about the lien process. Be sure to read it before agreeing to use a contractor for any of your work.

Cost You may think that using a subcontractor is never an economical idea. However, as a rental owner you have to remember that as long as a unit remains empty, you're losing money. It may cost you $400 to have a professional repair a bathroom floor and lay new vinyl. But, if he can do in a day what would take you a week or two, he's probably worth the $400. If you could be repainting the interior instead of working on the floor, your time would be more valuable there. Add the cost of specialized tools and equipment to the time you might save using a contractor, and you can see that hiring an expert to do a job often makes financial sense.

My contractor, who works for much less than he should, often recommends calling an expert. "The plumber can do this in half an hour," he'll tell me. "It would take me all day. And while he's doing that, we can get the other work done and have this place ready to rent by the end of the week."

To decide which choice makes sense, you will need to compare cost estimates. Until you have established a relationship with a couple of contractors, be sure to get at least three estimates for a job. Cost estimates often differ so widely that it's hard to know how to select among them. Sometimes a bidder submits a low estimate because the he doesn't understand the scope of the job. Or he might underbid consistently and hope to talk you into paying for cost overruns. Or he may be a poor businessman whose other poor practices may cause you problems.

High estimates are equally difficult to analyze. Again, the subcontractor may have misunderstood the scope of the job. Or he may have an inflated idea of his own skill. Or he may not want the job.

All in all, until you have some experience with costs in your area, it may be best to go with the mid-range estimate. Cost will be just one of the criteria you use to evaluate subcontractors. If the cost is high, but the person is dependable, fast, and produces high-quality work, you may consider it a bargain.

Estimates and Bids I asked my attorney one day to tell me what the difference was between a bid and an estimate. She said it was a "poorly defined area." No help there. To protect yourself, and to help your financial planning, insist on a written bid containing a complete description of the job. In some jobs, such as roofing, the quality of materials should also be specified. The bid should also include a paragraph outlining the contractor's guarantee of the quality of the workmanship, and your recourse if you're unhappy with it.

Scheduling The difficulty many subcontractors have returning phone calls and showing up when they agreed can come as a shock. Most of us are used to setting appointments and having everyone appear as scheduled. Independent contractors are a different subculture. They really emphasize the "independent." They don't work for anyone. They set their own schedules. And if you're lucky, they'll tell you what that schedule is, and maybe even stick to it.

I learned in the middle of a large project to call the contractors early in the morning to confirm that they really would be there at the appointed time. Before that, I'd pace and fume when they didn't show. The early call gave them less chance to swear that they forgot the appointment, or that I misunderstood the agreement.

I have a friend who has a sign on her mirror that says, "It's 7:30 a.m. Do you know where your contractor is?" Not a bad idea.

I think contractors tend to over commit when business is hot. They think they can do it all, and don't allow for time-consuming problems. Then, when they are running behind, they respond to the client who complains the loudest. You'll have to keep at them, loudly.

You can screen contractors the same way you screen other professionals. Asking specific questions of contractors makes your expectations clear. Their response to your questions also puts them on record.

Some questions for prospective contractors include:
- Are you licensed, bonded, and registered with the state?
- May I have three references, people you've done work for, to check?
- How do you calculate your bid? Will you discuss the numbers and your process with me?
- Tell me what circumstances might prevent you from finishing the work on time.

Screening contractors won't guarantee that you don't get the sort who leave for lunch and don't come back for three weeks, but it may help.

Back to Business: Record Keeping

If you think the rental business in general generates paper work, you haven't been through a fix-up yet. While it's going on you are sure you'll be nickel and dimed to death. Using a contractor or not, you'll make constant trips to the store for switch-plate covers, bolts to replace the ones that didn't fit, more paint, and a different screw driver. All those trips are tax deductible, as are the purchases. Be sure you record your mileage and keep all your receipts.

Ask your tax person how she likes to have mileage recorded. There are a number of ways to deal with it on your expense schedule. Also ask her about itemizing the supplies and materials. I try to write the rental unit address on the receipt when I make purchases. When I clean out my billfold, I throw the receipts into the folder for my current year's taxes. At the end of the year I sort the receipts out into

> *The time to repair the roof is when the sun is shining.*
> JOHN F. KENNEDY

piles by address. Then I add my totals to the ones generated by the property manager. The total goes straight on the tax form.

When you have a number of rentals, it can pay to have a business credit card you use only for expenses associated with your rentals. In this way, your statement reiterates the expenses and assures you that you haven't lost a receipt.

Analyzing a Fixer

If you have the time and the inclination, fixing up a property is rewarding. The transformation that takes place when you paint and landscape a run-down duplex is often enough to make you forget what a pain the process was at times. But the fun and the profit are available only when you've done your homework going in.

Realtors call the process of fixing up and selling either *turning* a property or *flipping* it. In the right market, flipping properties can be a good way to build up capital to get into larger rental units.

Analyzing a Fixer Property for Flipping

Be wary of Realtors who gush about the tremendous amount of money to be made on a fixer-upper. My real estate instructor likes to say that properties bought as fixers are most often resold as fixers. Lots of people get stung on them because they underestimate the cost of the fixing and their tolerance for the process. Let's look at some numbers for a flipper property

Jackie found a fixer listed at $115,000 in a desirable neighborhood. The home was outdated and had been neglected for some time. It had ceiling heat, which was no longer popular in the area, badly stained wood floors, landscaping trashed by three large dogs, three bedrooms with only a bath and a half, and the ugliest yellow and turquoise kitchen you ever saw.

The house also had 1600 square feet of well-configured living space, a huge yard, and no serious structural or mechanical problems except for the need for a heating system.

To figure out a price she would offer for the property, Jackie calculated the fix-up cost. Then she decided that she wanted a three-to-one ratio of dollars profit to dollars she invested. She added her selling costs, her required profit, and her fix-up cost to reach the numbers shown in the example.

To determine a possible sales price for the fixed-up property, Jackie attended several open houses in the neighborhood. She concluded the house she wanted would sell for around $165,000 when fixed up. She estimated her selling cost would be eight percent of the selling price, including six percent to a Realtor and another two percent for title insurance and pro-rated costs.

To estimate the cost of fixing up the house, Jackie went to her cost file. She added up all the cost of the work to be done, then multiplied that number by three. Remember, she wanted three dollars back for every one she spent on the fix-up.

Here is Jackie's estimate of costs:

```
Heating system  . . . . . . . . . . . . . . .$4,000
Interior paint (material)  . . . . . . . . . . .200
Floor (refinish)  . . . . . . . . . . . . . . . . .2,500
Vinyl (kitchen/bath) . . . . . . . . . . . . . .900
Kitchen
    counters (tile/oak trim)  . . . . . . . . . .150
    appliances (refinish)  . . . . . . . . . . . .450
    sinks/faucets  . . . . . . . . . . . . . . . . .400
    cabinets  . . . . . . . . . . . . . . . . . . . .850
Interior doors (6-panel)  . . . . . . . . . . .150
Light fixtures  . . . . . . . . . . . . . . . . . .300
Exterior door  . . . . . . . . . . . . . . . . . .300
Carpet . . . . . . . . . . . . . . . . . . . . . .2,000
Exterior paint  . . . . . . . . . . . . . . . . .1,500
Landscaping  . . . . . . . . . . . . . . . . . .500
Miscellaneous (10%) . . . . . . . . . . . .1,400
Subtotal  . . . . . . . . . . . . . . . . . .$14,600

Times 3 for profit  . . . . . . . . . . . . . .42,000
plus 8% sales cost . . . . . . . . . . . . .13,200
Total . . . . . . . . . . . . . . . . . . . . . .$55,200
```

If Jackie thinks she can sell the house for $165,000, she will need to pay $55,200 less than that for it.

Some notes about Jackie's estimates: She expected to do the interior painting, the kitchen tile work, and the cabinetry painting herself. Because this was an upscale home, she decided to buy new factory-finished cabinet doors for the kitchen. She also decided to replace the hollow-core interior doors with six-panel doors and to add a classy front door.

Unfortunately the seller countered Jackie's offer of $109,800 by asking for $114,000. Because Jackie thought her offer included a bare margin for potential unexpected problems she might encounter in the rehab work, she refused to increase her offer, and sadly turned down the deal. She later discovered that the dry rot in the kitchen was far more extensive than she had realized and counted herself lucky that she had refused to increase her offer.

Analyzing a Fixer Property for Rental René looked at an older building near a college campus. It contained seven rental units—five one-bedroom units and two studios. The one-bedroom units rented at $400 and the studios for $325 for a scheduled gross income of $31,800 per year. The building was in fairly good shape, needing mostly cosmetic work.

René's list of improvements looked like this:

Interior paint	$ 420
Carpet	3,000
Landscaping	400
Vinyl	2,800
Roof	3,000
Appliances (1/apt)	3,150
Total	**$12,777**

René calculated that the fix-up would allow her to increase rents $50 in the one-bedroom units and $25 in the studios. The increased rent would produce an additional $3,600 gross rent each year. The money René invested to fix up the property would be paid off in 3.6 years, well within René's time frame and goals. She bought the property, fixed it up, and now enjoys additional cash flow.

Don't underestimate the impact of cute or classy on a prospective renter. Designer touches may not raise the rent much, but they often reduce the time that a unit is vacant. In one of my vintage complexes the manager puts a sign up as soon as a move-out notice is received. The new renter is almost always someone who was walking by and saw the sign. Renters like the neighborhood and the charm of the old building. We seldom have to advertise to fill vacancies in this building.

Hiring professionals to help you fix up distressed properties can make financial sense. You do need to take care to find good contractors, make your expectations known, then supervise the work. You will have invested both time and money in finding a fixer that will return a solid profit to you. Don't let that profit slip through your hands by accepting unprofessional building help.

Summary

- ✔ Using contractors for some fix-up jobs can make financial sense.
- ✔ Get written bids, quotes, or estimates from at least three contractors.
- ✔ Interview prospective contractors carefully. Make your expectations clear.
- ✔ Analyze the costs of fixing up carefully, before you commit to a fixer.
- ✔ Remember, numbers for a flipper will be different from the numbers for a fix-and-hold rental.
- ✔ Keep environmental hazards in mind when looking at or working on a fixer.

■ *On the Internet*

One niche to consider as you fix up a property is that of older renters who may need barrier-free housing. For information, try the AARP website at **www.aarp.org/universalhome** and **www.design.nesu.edu/cud**

Chapter 15

Just for Women:
You Can,
You Should
Own Rentals

Luck is a matter of preparation meeting opportunity.
OPRAH WINFREY

Jennifer Openshaw, author of *What's Your Net Worth?*, reports that 75 percent of the elderly poor are women. Most of these women get by on Social Security checks of $600 or less a month. The situation is only slightly better for many women who are still employed.

- Women still make less than men—about 72 cents for every dollar.
- Women are out of the workforce an average of 11.5 years for care giving.
- Women are less likely to have an employer-sponsored pension plan.

In May 2002 an AFL-CIO survey found that adequate retirement income was the first priority of the women surveyed. Clearly, women need supplemental incomes both before and after they retire. Owning rental property can add to the income of the 58 percent of women who work and who rated their incomes as poor, as well as those who would otherwise depend on Social Security for their retirement.

The Mistakes Many of Us Make

Why do women find themselves in such poor financial condition as they age? Emily Card, publisher of *Emily Card's Moneyletter for Women*, identifies seven mistakes women make that cripple their long-term financial health. The following is adapted from Volume 1, Number 1. Are you making these mistakes?

1. *Expecting someone else to take care of your future financial needs.* Whether or not you are married, you need to know exactly what your financial status is. In 40 percent of American households, the woman is the primary breadwinner. But even in these households, the woman frequently does not know all there is to know about the family finances. Further, death or divorce can change a comfortable financial future to one of destitution overnight. The average woman's standard of living drops 45 percent in the year following divorce, while a man's standard of living rises 15 percent. Too many of us don't consider the possibilities and plan to deal with our own finances.

2. *Not knowing where your money goes.* It is far too easy to kid yourself about what things actually cost, especially if you habitually use a credit card. In 2002, 52 percent of women reported that they were worried about the amount of credit card debt they were carrying.

I think women are often so focused on the day-to-day financial issues of life that we find it hard to take a long view. Retirement is the last thing on our minds. When the kids need school clothes or braces, out comes the credit card, and the immediate problem is taken care of. Then, at the end of the month, when the bill arrives, we wonder just what we could have spent all that money on.

3. *Failing to plan for retirement.* In 2002, men saved more than twice as much toward retirement as women. Even women's employment-retirement plans lag far behind, with women reporting an average of $11,000 in a 401K compared to men reporting an average of $25,000. Social Security is not enough to live on comfortably.

4. *Being afraid to take even small risks.* Many women over-estimate the risk of even small investments. Some of the difference in the tolerance for risk may be gender related. For every 100 baby girls born, there are 104 baby boys born. By the time we reach our early twenties, however, just 97 males survive for every 100 females. Whether because of gender or socialization, boys take more physical risks than girls, and those risks are often deadly. "Hey guys, watch this," is not something we hear very often from women.

The task, it seems to me, is for women to overcome our genetics and socialization—with regard to financial risk taking at least. Perhaps a way to start is to compare the risks in investing to the risks involved in not investing.

Throughout this book I've tried to show you ways to make your money grow in a manner that is reasonably safe and effective. The risk of doing nothing dramatically increases the odds that your "golden years" will be tarnished by poverty.

5. *Treating clothes as an investment.* Muriel Siebert, the first woman to buy a seat on the New York Stock Exchange, tells women to put away an amount of money each month that is equal to the cost of their largest clothing purchase. If we all did that, at least we could see a real link between clothing and investments. Otherwise we are just falling prey to marketers who spend enormous amounts of money trying to convince us that we should spend, spend, spend. We have to stop viewing professional wardrobes as investments. They are expenses.

6. *Failing to set financial goals.* Unless you develop a financial plan with specific written goals and checkpoints, you, like Alice, will wander in the wilderness. Thinking about money is hard for many of us. But avoiding the issue is a sure way to disaster.

You might try sneaking up on a plan by day dreaming about what you want your life to be like when you retire, or what you would do on your most desired vacation. Imagine what you would spend to enjoy that scene, then back into the numbers that tell you how much money you'll need to be able to enjoy your dream.

7. *Letting "math anxiety" stand between you and a solid financial plan.* Math anxiety is not limited to women, however, women tend to act more on the anxiety. That is, we allow our fear of simple arithmetic to stand in the way of researching investments and committing to investing.

As a way to move from math anxiety to at least a tolerance for numbers, look again at the table that shows you how the power of compound interest can grow your savings. Remind yourself that you don't have to understand the theory of any of the calculations involved with buying and owning rentals. The only idea for which you must have a deep, gut-level understanding is that *enough money is better than not enough money.*

I believe that owning a small rental can help move women from the ranks of destitute senior citizens to more comfortable retirements. Anyone can own rentals. And women are especially suited to owning them.

Women Can Own Rentals: Women Should Own Rentals

Women are homemakers, whether they are in relationships or not. If we can make homes for ourselves and our families, we can help make homes for other families.

Among couples buying homes, women make the majority of the decisions about which house to buy. So too, when a couple looks for a rental, it will usually be the woman who has the final say about what to rent. When a woman buys or remodels a rental, she often thinks about how it would feel to live in the unit. Women landowners are in synch with tenants.

A woman landowner thinks about the details that make a house livable:

- Is there enough light in the kitchen?
- Is there enough storage?
- Does the traffic flow take everyone through the kitchen to get from one part of the house to the other?
- How hard is it to get the groceries out of the car and into the kitchen?
- Are there safe places for kids to play?

Awareness of these issues helps women choose and maintain appealing rentals.

The first duplex I bought was designed so that the driveway also served as the walk to the front door. The developer skimped on the amount of concrete, making the drive too narrow for both cars and people. Then he planted a huge, prickly shrub right where the car door had to open. It was impossible to park a car, get out of it comfortably, and carry parcels into the unit. The only approach to the door was across the lawn, which had a muddy gully worn in it by November of every year.

Women often bring a well-developed sense of social consciousness to land owning. They can be more sensitive to issues of affordable housing. Their tendency to relate rather than compete allows women to be flexible about things such as negotiating deposits and allowing pets.

At the same time, women who are mothers get lots of practice establishing rules and enforcing them. For example, my first manager used to say to young tenants, "Clean means the way your mother would expect it to be clean."

Women want and need to supplement their incomes during their working years and to increase their retirement funds. Owning even one duplex can assure you a retirement of comfort rather than one of deprivation. The sooner you begin, the more comfortable that retirement will be.

> *Women understand living space better than most men I'm acquainted with.*
> JAY P. DeCIMA

Success Scenarios

As I said before, the way you structure your purchase—the amount you borrow, and the length of the loan—determine the month-to-month cash flow from your investment. Here are some ways different women have structured transactions to meet their needs.

Big Payments Susan is a well-paid executive who worries about the burnout rate in her profession. She planned for early retirement or career change by buying a triplex with just three percent down and financing the remainder for 15 years. Susan's payments are so large that she must contribute almost $200 each month just to meet the payments. She reasons that her job is secure—at least in the foreseeable future—and she can manage the extra $200 every month. At the end of 15 years, her upscale triplex will be paid off, and she can retire or change jobs knowing that the income from the rents will provide a base for her.

Enforced Saving   Sandy, a grocery store checker, received a $5,000 bequest from an aunt. Sandy knew herself well enough to realize that she would never again have $5,000 in cash. Rather than treating herself to the cruise she had long dreamed of, Sandy bought a modest duplex, which provides an average of $150 cash flow each month. If she saves the cash from the duplex, Sandy will have enough for a luxury cruise in three or four years. She will have the vacation of a lifetime and come home to an investment that still gives her cash flow while it increases in value and shelters her income from some taxes.

College Expenses   Janie is a single parent with a daughter about to leave for college. Tuition and fees alone will consume all the savings Janie put aside for her daughter's education. She must find some other way to finance the cost of room and board. Janie took out an equity line of credit on her home and put the money down on a small two-bedroom house in the town where her daughter will go to college. She expects her daughter to find a roommate who will share expenses and reduce the amount Janie pays on the mortgage. Then, when her daughter graduates, Janie can either sell the property, trade it up into a larger investment, or continue to rent it to college students. If her daughter had been forced to use student loans for some of her expenses, Janie could sell the house to help her pay off the loans.

Women, in particular, need supplemental income both during their work life and in retirement. Investing in small rental properties can provide for both those needs. And women are especially suited to owning and managing rentals.

Summary

✔ Women are still at an income disadvantage compared to men, and that disadvantage extends into retirement.

✔ A combination of bad habits and inaccurate perceptions contributes to many women's lack of retirement planning.

✔ Rental ownership is particularly suited to women. Their life experiences nearly always includes being a homemaker on some level.

■ *On the Internet*

Women's Financial Network at **www.wfn.com**

Emily Card's Money Letter for Women at **www.womenmoney.com**

The Institute for Equality in Marriage at **www.equalityinmarriage.com**

The Widow's Checklist at **www.wiser.heinz.org**

The Social Security benefit calculator at **www.ssa.gov**

Chapter 16 | # Bon Voyage

The longest journey starts with a single step.
ANONYMOUS

By the time you've read this far, you've obviously committed to taking control of your financial future. Further, I hope you are thinking about investing in rental properties. One of the most important efforts you can make early in your career is to communicate your goals to your friends and family. You will need they active support for maximum success.

Get Everyone on Board

People have different tolerances for the risks they perceive in investing in rentals. Friends, family members, and significant others can throw up numerous roadblocks to your investment plans, especially if they have not been included in the planning. Even if they have been included, you may find that your views of the appropriate strategies differ.

There are no easy solutions to a situation where your spouse or partner disagrees with your investment strategy. But there are probably solutions. If you want to pursue a more aggressive strategy than your partner is comfortable with, you might try out strategies that temper your more risky-seeming inclinations—borrow less, perhaps, or extend the maturity time on the loan.

If you need to alter the family's spending habits in order to amass cash to invest, the family must committed to making the plan work. Otherwise, they may see your budgeting efforts as an austerity program with no payoff for them Try challenging the family to save a certain amount, or to have enough cash to buy a rental by a certain time.

If you want to try rehabbing, enlist your family and get them to share your enthusiasm. A serious rehab project is close to a full-time job. If you have a day job, you may find that you have little time to share with the family. Helping with the rehab work provides time to be together as well as more hands to lighten the load.

Recruiting family members to help with the work may make them feel like slaves in a project over which they have little control. If you expect the family to help drive screws into the sheetrock, be sure they also get to help with decisions about what property to buy, and what color to paint the walls.

Educate Everyone   Get your kids involved in financial discussions. If you are kicking yourself about not having started an investment plan 20 years ago, show the kids how different your financial position would be now if you owned a free and clear duplex.

What's Holding You Back?

The roadblocks to investing are often of our own making. I think the most common are these:

- Fear of risk.
- Lack of support from partners and family.
- Lack of cash.
- Fear of the unknown.

I hope this book has given you some ideas about how to deal with every one of these roadblocks. If you are still nervous about making the leap, go back to the appropriate chapters and read them again to psych yourself up. Go to the web site shown on the cover for more timely hints.

One Final Push

In condensed form, this is your step-by-step road map to financial independence:

- Outline your investment goals.
- Define your investment strategies.
- Evaluate your purchasing capacity; get a loan approval.
- Find property that fits your criteria.
- Purchase a property using one of the strategies you have worked out.
- Hold and rent that property until a time that makes sense for you to refinance it or sell it using either an exchange or paying the capital-gains tax on sale.
- Repeat as necessary to move along your pathway to financial freedom.

Now Go For It!
Bon Voyage!

Glossary

Adjustable rate mortgage (ARM) A mortgage loan that allows the interest rate to be changed at specific intervals over the maturity of the loan.

Amortize, amortization To pay off a loan with monthly payments that include a portion of the principal and one-twelfth of the annual interest.

Appreciation The increase in value of an investment over the cost.

Balloon payment A large lump-sum payment due on a regularly amortized loan prior to its normal maturity.

Binder An agreement, often accompanied by a deposit, to follow a particular course of action. An insurance binder demonstrates a buyer's commitment to pay the hazard insurance premium on a purchase, usually at closing.

Capitalization rate (cap rate) The rate at which investors are willing to invest capital. One indicator of value. Cap rate equals the net operating income divided by the market value.

Cash flow The amount of cash left after all the expenses and debt service payments have been made. Cash flow can be calculated either before or after income taxes have been subtracted.

Closing The act of transferring title to a property from a seller to a buyer. Also, the time when the closing takes place.

Closing costs The various costs associated with the transfer of title to real property, paid by the buyer and the seller at closing, the time of title transfer.

Compound interest The interest calculated on the sum of the original principal plus accrued interest.

Contract deed A written document which, when properly signed and recorded, conveys title to real property. Several kinds of deeds exist: warranty deeds, quitclaim deeds, and special warranty deeds.

Debt service The annual principal and interest payment on a loan, normally paid in monthly installments.

Deferred Maintenance Physical depreciation due to lack of normal upkeep.

Down payment The amount of cash paid by the buyer to the seller at the time of purchase.

Earnest money The deposit made by the purchaser of a piece of property as evidence of good faith in completing the purchase.

Easement The right held by person(s) B to property owned by person A.

Equity The difference between the fair market value of a property and the debt against that property.

Exchanging A method of trading one property for another that includes favorable capital-gains tax treatment made possible under Section 1031 of the Internal Revenue Code.

Fiduciary relationship A relationship of trust and confidence where one person acts as agent for another person, particularly in financial affairs.

Financial leverage Borrowing money at one rate and investing that money at a higher rate of return.

Gross income multiplier (GRM) The sales price of a property divided by the scheduled rent.

Hazard insurance Insurance that protects against loss from fires, floods, storms, and other damaging events.

Illiquid investment An investment that is difficult to convert into cash.

Improvements   The buildings or other structures erected on a piece of land.

Installment sale   Any sale of property where the payment is made in installments that span more than one year.

Liquidity   The ease with which an investment can be turned into cash.

Licensee   A person who holds a real estate sales or brokerage license.

Loan to value ratio (LTV)   The ratio of the amount borrowed to the market value of a property.

Prepayment clause, prepayment penalty   Fees charged to a borrower for paying off a loan prior to maturity.

Prime rate   The interest rate charged by banks to their best customers.

Realtor   A licensed real estate agent who belongs to and subscribes to the code of ethics of the National Association of Realtors. The term Realtor is a licensed trademark.

Recording   The act of entering into the public records information about the seller and the buyer of real property. Recording gives notice to the world of the facts of a transaction.

Refinancing   Taking out a new loan for the purpose of paying off the old loan.

Sweat equity   Work to be done by the borrower to increase the value of the property, usually in lieu of cash.

Tax shelter   An investment in which a portion of the return comes from realizing tax savings on other income as well as the receipt of tax-free cash flow from the investment.

Appendix

- **A Condensed APOD**

- **Sample Financial Statement**

- **Return on Investment Calculations**

- **Mortgage Principal and Interest Payment Factors Per $1,000 of Mortgage**

- **References**

Annual Property Operating Data—APOD

Rental owners classify their investments as *performing* (meeting cash flow expectations) or *nonperforming* (failing to meet cash flow expectations). The owners track the performance of their investment by calculating cash flow, depreciation, and return on equity. Each performance item is based on rents and expenses. The computations begin with the Annual Property Operating Data form. The sample form below computes cash flow from one of Caitlin's duplexes.

■ A Condensed APOD

	Caitlin	You
1. Scheduled gross income	$ 12,000	_____
2. Less vacancy allowance (5%)	(600)	_____
3. **Gross operating income** (Line 1 minus line 2)	**$ 11,400**	_____
Annual operating expenses 4. Maintenance/cleaning, management	1,600	_____
5. Property taxes	515	_____
6. **Total expenses** (Add lines 4 and 5)	**$ 2,115**	_____
(several other steps are skipped here)		
7. **Net operating income** (subtract line 6 from line 3)	**$ 9,285**	_____
Cap rate (line 7 divided by sales price)	**9.3 %**	_____

Some people own their rental free and clear, and others pay various mortgage payments. So the debt service is not one of the expenses used to calculate net operating income. The cash flow calculation, however, takes into account the debt service. Here is how Caitlin ended up with much less cash flow than Jessica.

	Caitlin	You
8. Net operating income (line 7)	$ 9,285	_____
9. Minus loan payments	(7,524)	_____
10. **Cash flow** (before taxes)	**$ 1,761**	_____

■ A Sample Financial Statement

Caitlin Nakamura
March 2001

Assets

Cash (First National Bank — checking)	$ 1,000
Cash (certificates of deposit)	2,500
Automobile (1998 Toyota)	10,000
Personal residence	130,500
Personal property (sports equip, furniture)	15,000
Total assets	$ 149,000

Liabilities

Mortgage on personal residence	$ 95,000
Line of credit (credit union)	15,000
Auto loan	2,000
Total liabilities	$ 112,000

Net worth (total assets minus total liabilities)	$ 37,000

■ Return on Investment Calculations

	Jessica 1 Duplex	Caitlin per Duplex
1. Invested	$100,000	$ 25,000
2. Loan	-0-	75,000
3. Gross rents	12,000	12,000
4. Expenses	3,000	3,000
5. Debt service	-0-	7,524
6. Cash flow	9,000	1,476
7. Depreciation	2,364	2,364
8. Increased market value	7,000	7,000
9. Principal reduction	-0-	4
10. Tax savings from depreciation	672	672
11. Return on investment	**17%**	**37%**

● Debt Service for $75,000 loan at 8% for 20 years is $672 per month per duplex (see next page for table of factors).

● Depreciation is calculated only on the improvements (buildings). Using a property tax statement to find the distribution of value between land and improvements shows the duplexes to be assessed at 65 percent for the improvements and 35 percent for the land. Therefore, $65,000 of the value of a $100,000 duplex is in the buildings. The IRS considers a 27.5 year life span for the improvements. With a 27.5 year lifetime, each building depreciates 1/27.5 of its value each year, or $2364.

● The tax savings is calculated by taking your marginal tax rate—most likely 28 percent—of the depreciation. In this case 28% of $2,364 is $662.

● The total return on investment is calculated by adding the tax savings, the cash flow, the appreciation, and the principal reduction together and dividing by the total amount invested. For Caitlin that is $662 + $1,476 + $7,000 + $4 which equals $9,142. $9,142 divided by the $25,000 she invested is 0.3657. To express as a percent, multiply by 100, that is, about 37%.

■ *Mortgage Principal and Interest Payment Factors Per $1,000 of Mortgage*

Suppose, for example, you are looking at a $250,000 loan at 5.5 percent for 20 years. What would the monthly loan payment be?

The multiplying factor to use is across from the interest rate and under the term in the chart below. The factor for this example is 6.88. It applies to each $1000 of loan. $250,000 is 250 thousand dollars. 250 x 6.88 = 1,720. The monthly payment for principal and interest would be $1,720.

Interest rate	15-year term	20-year term	30-year term
5.00%	7.91	6.60	5.37
5.25%	8.04	6.74	5.53
5.50%	8.17	6.88	5.68
5.75%	8.31	7.02	5.84
6.00%	8.44	7.17	6.00
6.25%	8.58	7.31	6.16
6.50%	8.72	7.46	6.33
6.75%	8.85	7.61	6.49
7.00%	8.99	7.75	6.65
7.25%	9.13	7.90	6.82
7.50%	9.27	8.06	6.99
7.75%	9.41	8.21	7.16
8.00%	9.56	8.36	7.34
8.25%	9.70	8.52	7.51
8.50%	9.85	8.68	7.69
8.75%	9.99	8.84	7.78
9.00%	10.14	9.00	8.05

■ *References*

● Johnson, Stacy.
Life or Debt: A One-Week Plan for a Lifetime of Financial Freedom

● Gardner, David and Tom Gardner.
The Motley Fool, You Have More Than You Think

● Irwin, Robert.
How to Get Started in Real Estate Investing

● Openshaw, Jennifer.
What's Your Net Worth: Click your Way to Wealth

● Stone, Martin, and Spencer Strauss.
The Unofficial Guide to Real Estate Investing

● Kiyosaki, Robert T. & Sharon L. Lechter.
Rich Dad, Poor Dad

● Janik, Carolyn.
Making Money in Real Estate: How to Build Financial Independence with Residential and Commercial Property

● Bach, David.
Smart Women Finish Rich

● Stanley, Thomas J. and William D. Danko.
The Millionaire Next Door

● DeCima, Jay P.
Investing in Fixer-Uppers

Acknowledgements

Significant life changes are often the culmination of years of subconscious processing. I'm fortunate to have the chance to thank friends and mentors for their support of that process, and to the writing about it.

Thanks to Bob Nelson who introduced me to rentals, and has mentored each step. Thanks to René Nelson and Linda O'Bryant who help keep me up to date about rental and mortgage markets.

Thanks to Joy Poust and Christina Newman who taught me what a well-run property-management firm should do, and Brian Tuske and Chris Frey who continued my education. Thanks to Jim Calkins who sets the standard for property maintenance and is always ready for a new remodel project.

My writing support groups, Val Brooks, Skye Blaine, Candy Davis, Carol Craig, and Elizabeth Lyon deserve credit for the direction this book took, but none of the blame for the inevitable mistakes herein.

Thanks also to the Thursday snack-bunch: Bobbye Sorrels, Martha Bayless, and Vickie Nelson. Especially to Vickie who doubles as the world's greatest editor.

Finally, thanks to Robert, Jim, and Susan for your support and encouragement.

Index

■ *Order Form*

Give the gift of *How to Invest in Rental Properties Without Mortgaging Your Soul* to your friends and colleagues.

Yes, I want _____copies of *How to Invest in Rental Properties Without Mortgaging Your Soul.*

Send $19.95 per book, check or money order. Include $2.95 shipping and handling for one book, and $1.50 for each additional book.

My check or money order for $_____is enclosed.

Name _____

Address _____

City/State/Zip _____

Make your check payable to:

Stone Pine Press
PO Box 585
Marcola OR, 97454